Richard Adams

A Nature Diary

Illustrated by John Lawrence

Viking

VIKING
Penguin Books Ltd, Harmondsworth, Middlesex, England
Viking Penguin Inc., 40 West 23rd Street, New York, New York 10010, U.S.A.
Penguin Books Australia Ltd, Ringwood, Victoria, Australia
Penguin Books Canada Ltd, 2801 John Street, Markham, Ontario, Canada L3R 1B4
Penguin Books (N.Z.) Ltd, 182–190 Wairau Road, Auckland 10, New Zealand

First published 1985

Set in Dante
Printed and bound in Great Britain by
William Clowes Limited, Beccles and London

Colour reproduction by
Brian Gregory Associates Ltd., St. Albans, Herts.

Designed by Elizabeth Ayer

British Library Cataloguing in Publication Data

Adams, Richard, 1920–
    Nature diary.
    1. Natural history——England
    I. Title
    574.942   QH138

    ISBN 0–670–80105–4

Library of Congress Catalog Card Number: 84–52016

To the memory of my father,
Evelyn George Beadon Adams, F.R.C.S.
(1870–1946)

O mihi praeteritos referat si Iuppiter annos.
(*Aeneid*, Book VIII)

Acknowledgements

I acknowledge with thanks the invaluable help I have received from Clif Dadd, Ronald Lockley and Jonathan Quick and express my sincere gratitude to Mrs Elizabeth Aydon and Mrs Janice Kneale, who typed the manuscript.

For the origin of Tetter's name see *Hamlet* I, v, 71–2.

Introduction

It may be helpful and spare some readers disappointment to explain what this book is and is not meant to be. It is not a catalogue of rare and seldom-seen things, but an authentic day-to-day record made during a calendar year at home in the Isle of Man, with various short visits to England, Wales, Denmark and Australia. Apart from the Anglesey bird-watching course in July, there were no deliberate 'nature-watching' expeditions. I simply wrote down what I saw or heard every day. I should add, also, that since I have no specialized natural history qualifications, I enlisted expert help to check accuracy as regards nomenclature.

Anyone, therefore (with a little application and a few standard reference books on birds, flowers, etc.), could keep a nature diary on the same lines as this. I hope it may stimulate more amateurs like me to try their hand, for the project has been very enjoyable. There is a moral here, but rather than spell it out I will tell a little story.

Some years ago, when I used to work in Whitehall (where there wasn't all that much nature to be observed), I used to enjoy seeing the flocks of starlings come in to roost at sunset. Attracted by the warmth of central London, they would arrive from the country in thousands, and strut and tussle along the office buildings for their pendent beds and procreant cradles for the night. One evening I was standing near a window in the Old Treasury Building near Horse Guards Parade, discussing some civil service matter with two people from another Department whom I didn't know very well. Suddenly the starlings began to arrive. The air outside became darkly alight with wings and with squabbling and cackling, but after a few minutes, while our talk continued, things became a bit quieter.

'I like to see the starlings come in, don't you?' I remarked to one of my companions.

'Starlings?' he replied, puzzled and slightly put out, for I had broken his train of thought.

'Several thousand starlings,' said I, 'have just alighted rather noisily within a few yards of us.'

'Oh – really?' he replied, and for a split second he and the other fellow caught each other's eyes. Then he resumed where I had interrupted him.

I must add that we weren't all like that. A colleague once dumped six different kinds of fungi on my desk and asked rather dauntingly, 'Can you identify those?' (*He* could.)

This book, then – apart from being meant for amusement – is merely intended to illustrate how much free enjoyment anyone can derive from simply keeping his or her eyes open in going about normal daily affairs. I admit I have the advantages of living in the country and of working in my own time. Those, perhaps, may give this diary a bit of extra depth; but a lot of the things in it – the stars, for example, and many of the birds and wild flowers – are no more than can be seen by anyone.

Any authentic diary (like Parson Woodforde's) is rather like watching cricket; it is bound to have its *longueurs*. But just as, to the true enthusiast, there is always much to observe and appreciate, even when a side is playing for a draw, so there is always something to enjoy in nature, even in January or November. Keeping an eye on nature isn't really a matter of going out looking for rarities. When I got to know Ronald Lockley, that fine naturalist, I discovered (and it surprised me, then) that if there was nothing else about he was perfectly happy to watch sparrows. He liked them as he liked all birds. Similarly, my father, a country doctor, sometimes used to pick a dandelion and put it in his buttonhole. He enjoyed the way the colours vary, across the bloom, from yellow to deep orange. It was he who first pointed them out to me.

Here, then, is my very ordinary nature diary. Anyone who finds it dull has a simple and pleasurable recourse – to keep his own.

January

1ST JANUARY

Determined that this diary should start off with a bit of a flourish,
I sallied forth on this fine winter's day to see what I could find in
bloom. The answer was, quite a lot. Gorse, ragwort, several
dandelions, some hogweed and yarrow, a whole lot of red campion
(rather washed-out), a daisy (*Bellis perennis*); and, surprisingly, near
the stone quarry beside the Poortown road, several ox-eye daisies
(*Chrysanthemum leucanthemum*). In a cottage garden down by the
river Neb, a laurustinus in more-or-less full bloom, a bush of
purple veronica, some silvery wormwood in yellow flower (smelt
nice) and a clump of pink *Oxalis articulata*. There was some kind
of cultivated heather blooming there, too. But best of all, on the
waste patch outside my own gate, there was what had every
business to be in bloom – a good, big patch of *Petasites fragrans*,
the pink winter heliotrope. (A butterbur, I note; whereas true
heliotrope is a borage.) I don't know a more beautifully scented
wild flower. I went down on my knees to snuff it – like F. T. Prince
in his poem – and then brought some in to put on the library
table.

9

Since Clif Dadd, our horticultural expert, treated the slope below the house with weed-killer as a prologue to laying out the new garden later this year, I thought the goldfinches would lose interest in us. (No more thistle or burdock seeds.) But not a bit of it! A charm of three (do three make a charm? They charmed me, anyway) came bouncing in this morning. They must be the prettiest birds going. You'd wonder John Clare never wrote about them: at least, I can't find that he did. But Keats has some lovely lines in 'I Stood Tiptoe'. Burns called goldfinches, rather strangely, 'music's gayest child'. The only whole poem I know is Cowper's sad and telling 'On a Goldfinch Starved to Death in its Cage'.

Country names for the goldfinch: King Harry, Spotted Dick, Sheriff's Man, Foolscoat, Sweet William, Jack Nicker. And there's a village in Normandy called Sainte-Honorine-La-Chardonnerette.

3RD JANUARY

Much colder to-day. Stewart Kneale (husband of my secretary, Janice) and I walked along the disused railway line and back down the beach below Kirk Michael. A beautiful, grey sunset; grey sky, grey sea and a new moon setting over Peel Castle. Later, as we were returning to Onchan over the top above Druidale, a white mountain hare (*Lepus timidus scoticus*) came out of the heather on to the road, paused in the headlights and was gone like a ghost.

4TH JANUARY

Out in the rain this afternoon. Coming down a stubbly pasture not a furlong from the sea, I put up a big flock of small birds. They were indistinct against the waning light and I wondered what they could be. Certainly not starlings – wrong flight behaviour and too small. Not meadow pipits either – they didn't flirt in flight. Then, at the further edge of the field, I came upon three sitting on a wire and got my field-glasses on them. Greenfinches! Their little black domino masks were very clear.

5TH JANUARY

Adjacent to the northern boundary of my house, called 'Knocksharry', is some land belonging to the Manx Water Board. They have screened the installation with a thick belt of pines, and this attracts conifer-haunting birds. To-day I saw two tree-creepers. I'd forgotten how small they are – and how white-breasted. The book points out that they can 'creep' only *up* trees, and not both up and down, as nuthatches can. However, I can inform the book that they can certainly cling to the underside of a thick branch, like a fly on a ceiling, and work along it upside-down; because I've watched one doing so.

6TH JANUARY

A good walk this afternoon in bright sunlight and clear, frosty weather. Ros. (my younger daughter) dropped Tetter (my black-and-white border collie) and me at Glenmaye. We climbed Slieau Whallian by the lane, through the meadows and finally across the heath; then over the summit and down through the pine-woods to St John's; and so back to Knocksharry along the disused railway line. It took two hours and forty minutes, and I suppose it might be about seven and a half miles.

Tetter put up a jack snipe on Slieau Whallian, quite close to me in the sunshine. I was startled by the brilliance of its colouring; speckled chestnut and white. It must have gone twisting away a good five hundred yards before dropping into a patch of bogland lower down the mountain.

As I was coming along the disused railway line, there was a saffron sunset over Peel on the left; and on the right, a rising moon over the Greeba Ridge. Cat-ice shattered satisfyingly under the boots. Venus – what *The Times* calls 'a brilliant object in the western sky' – towards heaven's descent had sloped his westering wheel. (Wonder why Milton made Venus masculine? He must have known it was Venus? Carey and Fowler, however, his editors in the Longman edition, don't indicate that *they* do.) It certainly was a splendid sight in the fading ochre last light, and didn't set until an hour or so after the sun.

10TH JANUARY

Everything points to an early, mild spring. Of course, this is the Isle of Man, lapped by the Gulf Stream, but even so it's the kindest of weather for January. The evenings are perceptibly lengthening. It's ten past five now, and twilight; Venus setting, and a moist, leafy, earthy smell from the wood and the garden. The rooks clamouring about the Lhergy Dhoo (of which more anon) and Tetter anxious to get out walking. Primroses blooming – not many, but enough to notice – and a yellow wallflower. Also a snowdrop in bud.

Four miles later. I love a clear, cloudless night. You could smell the resinous pines and firs in the dark, and see the elm branches (thank goodness we still have our elms here) against the sky. Well-trained Tetter now completely obedient whenever a car approaches. He may be eighty yards ahead: 'Tetter! Stop!' and down he goes on the verge. A good dog is a comfort and a blessing.

11TH JANUARY

A hundred yards from Knocksharry, to the north, is the road junction of the Switchback and the Peel to Kirk Michael road. On the hillside rising above on the east stands a wood. This is the Lhergy Dhoo, which is Manx for the Black Hillside. I like to think it's so called because of the rookery. There has been a rookery here time out of mind. I love to hear the rooks going about their business: but then I'm not a farmer. These winter mornings they get up more or less when I do. I see them flying out field-wards in the grey, early light, drifting past like great cinders on the wind. At nightfall you can hear them cuckling and rarking together, up in the wood, until it's become dark and for some time after that. On fine summer evenings they sail round and round, high up in the last sunshine, cawing and gliding together. It seems unnecessarily anti-romantic to regard this as 'establishment of territorial rights'. Surely the truth is that they do it simply for their pleasure?

12TH JANUARY

Stewart couldn't come walking this afternoon, so Tetter and I set off to walk on the Greeba Ridge. It was misty along the top. I went what I reckoned was two miles southward and then turned, as I thought, east. After a bit I began descending and approached a beck. That beck should have been running from right to left. It was running from left to right. The light was failing and I decided to play safe and follow the beck down. After about a mile I realized I was 90° out – I'd been going south instead of east and had never been on the eastern side of the Ridge at all! Once I knew where I was, and being now below the mist, I simply turned back for the car. Climbing over a dry-stone wall on the near side of a beck, an envious sliver broke, and down my weedy trophies and myself – well, myself, anyway – fell in the weeping brook. I bruised my hip quite painfully, but I was lucky not to be banged about the ankles by the falling stones (which I replaced). Altogether, a trying two and a half hours. It just shows how unwise it is to go out walking in mist without a compass; and at only about 1,500 feet or less! Anyway, Tetter enjoyed it. All one to him, sir, in the way of the world.

13TH JANUARY

A still, windless, grey, subdued sort of day. Sunday dinner at Janice and Stewart's. Then we all three walked from Port Groudle along the cliff to Clay Head, inland to Baldrine and back by the lane past Lonan Old Church. Janice – who hadn't been out walking for some time – in excellent form and rainbow-coloured, knitted long socks: but rather nervous in fields of cows. Girls are, as a rule.

14TH JANUARY

Touched to receive a picture postcard to-day from Cliff, of 'The Spinners' folk song group, on holiday in Jamaica. How nice of him to think of me! I mind me, now, that he and I once had some talk of going to Jamaica together. To go to Jamaica in the company of a black Jamaican friend would open one's eyes and ears no end, I should think; and one would meet some fascinating people. Just another thing that might happen one day!

15TH JANUARY

From Knocksharry House due west to the sea (White Strand) is a shade over half a mile and from there to the summit of Slieve Donard (2,796 feet), the highest peak of the Mountains of Mourne in Ulster, is forty-five miles. Sometimes – as to-day – you can't see the Mountains from Knocksharry. At other times you can discern them if you know what you're looking for. Again, they rise out of the sea so distinct and close that through binoculars you can pick out individual features clearly. They are particularly beautiful when snow is lying, or when the sun sets behind them and shows them as a black mass against a fiery sky, fronted by a glowing sea.

16TH JANUARY

Some of the fishing boats from Peel, two miles away, often lie out at sea all night, their lights showing plainly through the dark. If I happen to get up in the night, I generally look out of the window to see whether they're there. Sometimes there may be half a dozen; sometimes none. On a night of full moon you can make out the boats themselves, but in darkness, of course, you see only the lights. This always has an oddly comforting and cheerful effect on

me. I observe that the image of a light in darkness has for centuries had this effect on people. (Reassuring, I suppose.)

'And the light shineth in darkness; and the darkness comprehended it not.' (John I, 5)

PORTIA: That light we see is burning in my hall.
How far that little candle throws his beams!
(*Merchant of Venice*, V, i)

It didn't have the same effect on Edward Lear, though. The Dong with a Luminous Nose was a sad, lonely creature out in the dark and wet.

Another odd thing; a *soft* light has this reassuring effect, but not a very bright one, which seems merely hard and intrusive.

17TH JANUARY

For Christmas Ros. gave me one of those Japanese miniature bonsai trees – an elm. It is exactly seven inches high to the top branch, with a girth at the base of an inch and a half. Its maximum breadth, 180° from the tip of one branch to the tip of the opposite branch, is five inches. At the moment it is a perfect miniature to scale and looks very healthy. I have placed it in one of the window embrasures in the library. Its leaf-buds are just showing. 'The lowest boughs and the brush-wood sheaf/Round the elm-tree bole are in tiny leaf.' Particularly tiny in this case. (It has no brush-wood sheaf.)

19TH JANUARY

A nice letter from Colin Wilson, saying he is writing a book on Astronomy. The Ordinary Man (whoever he is) could certainly do with one. I mean, an astronomical equivalent of Keble Martin on Wild Flowers. It's often puzzled me that lots of people who know about flowers and birds can't even pick out Perseus or recognize Capella. And yet stars give so much comfort and pleasure.

20TH JANUARY

At East Lhergy Dhoo Farm, about half a mile away, a rivulet runs down the field and then turns at right-angles along the ditch beside the lane. Here it makes a little, plashing fall into a tiny pool with a heavy, square, brick (Manx) gatepost above. In the bank, just above the water, are three beautiful, luxuriant hart's-tongue ferns (*Phyllitis scolopendrium*). This is the fern with undivided fronds, and brown scales along the stalks. If I were Beatrix Potter, I'd paint an immortal watercolour of someone like Mrs Tiggy-Winkle fetching water from that little pool below those ferns, their glossy, crinkled fronds overhanging the surface.

21ST JANUARY

In Ronald Blythe's book *The View in Winter*, a man who used to be a Duke's gamekeeper many years ago tells how 'His Grace loved ivy' and would have ivy, God help us, *deliberately* planted against every new tree! I can't bear to see a tree smothered in ivy! It's like that story I read somewhere, about the island where the castaways were gradually encrusted with a terrible, sponge-like fungus, until they no longer resembled human beings. Along the verge of the east end of the Poortown road and at Ballig Bridge, many of the ashes are completely overgrown with ivy. Several can hardly last much longer.

22ND JANUARY

I feel rather like an ornithological Mr Jorrocks. 'CON-found, say I, all crows vot makes life okkard for self-respectin' birds and them as vants to vatch 'em!' Many of my visitors like to see the hooded crows, which if they're southerners they haven't come across before. The rather striking pale-grey and black plumage takes their fancy. The fact is, we are infested with the darned things. They eat birds' eggs, and nestlings, too, if they can. But from my point of view, their worst crime is busting nut-bags. You buy a plastic-net bag of nuts and hang it up for the tits. The hooded crow flies at it very fast and hits it a terrific bang. If this doesn't work he does it again. Sooner or later the bag breaks and the nuts are strewn all abroad. Down goes the crow, driving everything else away, and eats them.

23RD JANUARY

Now jackdaws are another matter. I don't mind a good jackdaw, even though the book says that they too steal eggs and nestlings. They don't bust nut-bags, anyway, or hang around my property in a menacing way. I like to see them along the cliffs. There's something attractive about the round, white eye – sharp and knowing. When I was living at Ravensdale Castle, there was an old conservatory in the garden. It had a tall, brick chimney-stack – disused, of course – in which a pair of jackdaws built. It was delightful to see the male bird emerge, perch on the edge of the chimney-pot and look round with an air of being very clever. Then he'd go off to forage, return, perch again, turn head downward and descend vertically into the depths.

24TH JANUARY

On the rocks at Peel Castle this afternoon I saw a bird I couldn't identify or even begin to guess at. I did the only possible thing – watched it as long and closely as I could until 'twas in my memory locked. It was doing nothing in particular, and doing it very well. I rushed home and searched the book. It was a female snow bunting (*Plectrophenax nivalis*). The white breast was very noticeable.

25TH JANUARY

George Wedd arrived to-day. A three-day holiday from writing, and an excellent reason to open some good wine! George tells me of old friends and colleagues in Whitehall who all seem to have become pleasingly eminent. I reckon the most heart-warming function of friends is to talk the same language. George and I are light blue and dark blue, both history graduates, both Whitehall warriors with about a quarter of a century of local government experience. If *we* don't speak the same language I don't know who does.

The weather has suddenly become glorious – clear and frosty, with sunshine. This afternoon we walked from Peel Castle (George, at a glance, correctly guessed the curtain walls to be fifteenth century) along the cliffs to Glenmaye. Not a lot to be seen, unless you count a covey of ringed plovers flickering away over the sea, seen from 200 feet above. At Glenmaye we had a few pints in the Waterfall, after which we were given a lift back to Peel by charming Chris, the landscape-painting barmaid.

26TH JANUARY

The beautiful weather holds. (Saturday.) Pints at the Manx Arms, lunch with Stewart and Janice; then Stewart, George and I walked over Slieau Whallian. In spite of the sunny afternoon, visibility out to sea was poor. From the summit of Slieau Whallian you can see all coasts of the Island except the north. But that was all you *could* see.

We spent the evening drinking port and listening to Schubert, for whom George has great regard. Well, I have too, but one might have expected the shrewd, rather anti-romantic and at times sardonic George to lean rather towards e.g. Bach. I have a theory that taste in art is compensatory. E.g. in the sixteenth century life was harsh and messy, and what did they like in the way of poetry? Campion's lyrics and Spenser's faultless, predictable symmetry. To-day we lead hygienic, tidy lives; and painting, anyway, tends towards the abstract and primitive. Does Schubert give George what he *hasn't* got, or is it that for him Schubert reaches the spot other beers can't reach?

A calm night, entirely without wind. We all slept soundly.

27TH JANUARY

Another perfect day. Walked beside the secluded, arboriferous lower Neb this afternoon, from St John's to Peel. As we reached the broad, still, rather cavernous reach by the disused mill, a good three-quarters of a mile above the harbour, I saw a young cormorant, fishing on its own in the fresh water. We watched it for some time, swimming underwater. At first I thought it was a young shag, for I couldn't see a white face-patch. But both Dr Burton and *The A.A. Book of British Birds* emphasize that *unlike the cormorant*, the shag is confined to cliffs, rocky coasts and off-shore islands and never goes inland.

28TH JANUARY

This morning the mist could clearly be seen, spilling from seaward over the saddle south of Corrin's Hill. From Knocksharry, nearly four miles away, it looked like theatrical 'mist' being released, as at the close of Richard Rodney Bennett's terrifying *The Mines of Sulphur*. Throughout the morning it slowly advanced, until by lunch-time it was lying in Roy Callin's big meadow below the house.

George was due to leave by air at 5 p.m., but he never got off, because the whole south of the Island was under thick mist. I consoled him by taking him to the Castletown bookshop, where we each bought another Schubert record – he the string quintet in C major, I the Wanderer Fantasy. He didn't seem loath to stay another night. We listened to Schubert until well after midnight.

29TH JANUARY

After George had departed for London, I found he'd left the C major quintet in the library, for me.

It's rained all day. I did four miles with Tetter in a quiet drizzle. Numerous snowdrops are in bud and will soon be out. The dwarf cyclamen are shaping well beside our little waterfall. We have two or three bowls of indoor hyacinths in bloom.

30TH JANUARY

Anniversary of the execution of King Charles. 'I must be up betimes, for I have a great work to do this day.' Nothing in his life became him like the leaving it.

As my secretary, Janice, departed in her car at five o'clock this evening – fine, still weather – I heard a robin singing from the hawthorn hedge across the road, and realized I'd heard no bird-song for days past. Standing by the gate to signal Janice out, I saw Master Robin fly away up the hedge and as he did so an enormous, almost full moon rose slowly over the hill beyond.

Out of a monthly article of 116 lines only, the *Times* astronomical correspondent takes five to say this (of Orion): 'This bright constellation is far more than a mythological hunter facing the Bull, treading on the Hare and followed by the Dog Star.'

Just what is this supposed to tell us? He's wasted 4·31 per cent of a meagre monthly ration in taking a meaningless swipe at – what, exactly? Romantic star-gazers like me, I suppose. Orion will be a big feature of the early evening sky this month. Good. I enjoy looking at it, O *Times* astronomical correspondent, facing the Bull, treading on the Hare and followed by the Dog Star.

31ST JANUARY

To-day I've been watching the starlings. I have an affection for them. The plumage is beautiful against the light, and the quick, strutting walk is comical; but what I like most is the flight. Owing to the birds' relatively small size, their rapid wing-beat and habit of keeping close together when flying in flocks, they appear to flicker in flight in a characteristic and delightful way. The flocks are inexplicably unanimous, all turning together as one bird. Perhaps starlings are not really conscious of being individuals. Yet a flock, as it reaches height, will spray out this way and that, and single birds will break off.

They mob a kestrel by circling round it in numbers.

February

Injebreck below Carraghan

1ST FEBRUARY

My father's birthday. He died nearly thirty-four years ago. I loved
him dearly. How odd to reflect that he was born 110 years ago to-
day! Gladstone was Prime Minister, Livingstone was bashing his
way through Tanganyika; and Trollope, at fifty-four, published,
inter alia, his little book on Julius Caesar. As a boy in Somerset a
hundred years ago my father, so he once told me, was a dead shot
with a catapult. He said he much regretted how many little birds
he had shot. There is probably less *wanton* killing to-day, yet the
animals and birds are, by and large, worse off. It spoils the world,
that they have no rights.

2ND FEBRUARY

The miniature elm still looks healthy. The scent of the hyacinths
on my table seems as marvellous as if I'd never smelt a hyacinth in
my life before.

A light fall of snow last night – about an inch. It was very cold
in the bedroom when I woke, but I've yet to rival Parson
Woodforde's diary entry that the contents of the piss-pot froze
under the bed. The snow was all gone by tea-time. Tetter and I
sploshed four miles in gum-boots. (I wore the gum-boots.) Saw
little or nothing.

3RD FEBRUARY

Coal tits are common with us – commoner than blue tits. I suppose they like the conifers round the house. They never keep still for a moment. Len Howard, in her book *Living with Birds*, records that she never succeeded in domesticating any coal tits, although she had the house swarming with blue tits and great tits.

5TH FEBRUARY

The aconites are out, and a few snowdrops. One plant of the dwarf cyclamen has a bloom in bud.

All the same, thought I this evening, how does a nature diarist wax enthusiastic about slogging uphill through a field of mangel-wurzels in mud, gathering darkness and rain? Tetter, however, enjoyed every minute; and took a deal of drying when we got home. He likes being dried, holding up each paw of his own accord.

6TH FEBRUARY

Of all the signs of coming spring, I think my favourite – as good as snowdrops – is to hear the great tit 'ringing his bell'. He takes a high song-post, and this in itself is exhilarating, for he seems to want the whole world to hear him. The little, repeated phrase – '*hi*-chicker, *hi*-chicker' – is a very cheerful sound.

7TH FEBRUARY

In a field west of Kirk Michael this afternoon I counted seventeen live lambs and one dead 'un. They're early, of course – 'brought on' by artificial means. Still, the weather can be just as severe in March. I can't see that it's any harder for them now.

8TH FEBRUARY

This evening I reckon I can fairly claim to have had a major ornithological experience. I was coming in the car from the Injebreck reservoir, past Injebreck House (a mass of snowdrops in front – most beautiful) and up on to Injebreck Hill above. It was lonely on the moor, with Colden rising steeply above. Dusk was falling in windy drizzle and a lot of low, driving mist. Suddenly, out of the mirk, three ravens came flying towards me, just below where the wind-pleached beeches line one side of the road. They alighted less than a hundred yards to my right, among the heather. They looked enormous – unmistakable; I saw their 'beards' quite distinctly.

I stopped the car and began to approach them. It was like *Macbeth* – gathering darkness, fog and filthy air and these three great brutes hopping and capering grotesquely on the moor. When I was about fifty yards from them they rose heavily and flew off eastward, being soon lost to view.

9TH FEBRUARY (*Saturday*)

I have picked up a cold which has gone to the chest. 'I can't get be'ind it, doctor', as the old age pensioners used to say to my father. After lunch I felt so rotten that I went to bed. Good Philip Christian (our doctor) turned out to come and see me at home, at nine o'clock on a Saturday evening. He gave me some anti-biotics, which helped a lot. I must give *him* a bottle of whisky or some appropriate token of esteem. How our doctors show up American doctors! When I was teaching at Gainesville, five years ago, not one doctor in the town would come, on a weekday morning, to the bedside of one of my pupils with a temperature of 103°. 'Doctor Hokeypoke don't make domiciliaries,' barked the 'lady' receptionists I telephoned. No wonder the Americans hate and distrust their doctors! Philip gets nothing extra for coming to see me at home on a Saturday evening, at no notice whatever.

10TH FEBRUARY (*Sunday*)

In bed all day. Pleased to observe one cock pheasant and two hens evidently resident on the property.

11TH FEBRUARY

Philip called again this morning. I gave him a bottle of Glenlivet. I'm to stay indoors till Thursday and remain on anti-biotics. Reading: (i) *Paradise Lost*, (ii) Gittings's *Life of Keats*, (iii) *Nana*. They all seem very good, as the man said.

Elizabeth (my wife) took Tetter three miles this afternoon and came back with a twig of ribes (flowering currant) covered with leaf-buds. It smells marvellous! (Janice says it smells like tom-cats.) Anyway, I can smell the ribes – I can smell the hyacinths – I can't be very bad. I wish I could get be'ind it, though. I feel quite tired with coughing.

12TH FEBRUARY

Consolations of being not very well. First, on Radio 3, 'This week's composer' – Rachmaninov. How splendid! Secondly, a fascinating short article by Richard Gulliver, in *Country Life*, on the flora and fauna of disused railway lines. We've got enough of those here. I must see whether I can ratify some of his points. The basic one is that cuttings and embankments used to be cut short, and this encouraged e.g. the dwarf thistle, and ants' nests. On disused lines, in the wake of bramble come hawthorn and elder; willow warblers, whitethroats, voles, woodmice, kestrels, etc.

13TH FEBRUARY

'Better to-day. Better to-day,' said Lord Marchmain. (But he wasn't.) I am. But don't these anti-biotics make you dream? – or something

does. I woke at four in the morning to hear the curlews calling in the night. The sheep were quietly grazing in Roy Callin's big field just as though it were day, and the distant harbour lights of Peel were shining in the solitude.

14TH FEBRUARY

(St Valentine's Day, All in the morning betime.) The topmost branches of the sallows are now plainly in grey shoot. In other words, the first pussy willow is here! *Salix caprea*, found everywhere in damp woodlands, scrub and hedges. Alan Mitchell: 'The native sallows are a complex group and several species, sub-species and hybrids occur, most of which pass as "pussy willow" when in flower.' This one's a good thirty-five feet tall – one we spared when Clif Dadd felled the scrubby bog to start making the lake. It has a lovely, moss-covered base.

Making the lake – this is going to be exciting!

Mere rhapsodizing about weather, nature, etc., is boring. None the less, it's hard to refrain to-day. The first day of spring – though no doubt we'll have more hard weather later. Bright, warm sunshine, no wind and naturally everyone very cheerful – including a chaffinch singing his little, falling phrase again and again.

thuidium
tamariscinum

I wasn't supposed to go out of doors until to-morrow, but the weather being so exciting, I walked up Glen Helen to the ruined Keeill (medieval chapel, hermitage, monk's cell or whatever) at the top, and back again; two miles.

I observed: bluebells shooting; montbretia shooting in light green, delicate spears, only an inch or two high. (It grows wild everywhere here.) Honeysuckle well on in leaf. Two ferns: (i) *Polypodium interjectum*, growing in a crevice; (ii) *Blechnum spicant*, the hard fern. Both common enough, but being a Berkshireman and not coming from fern country, I always like to see wild ferns.

The most delightful thing in the glen – I have a saucerful on my desk now – was *Thuidium tamariscinum* – the fern moss, as I call it. I've been puzzling over the book, which says: 'The main stems are branched three times in a very regular manner, and the leaves on the branches are smaller and narrower than those on the main stems.' Sounds plain enough, but I can't *see* it, either in the picture or in the saucerful itself: yet I'm in no doubt of the identification.

~ the ruined Keeill ~

In the library this morning, I noticed what looked like a medium-sized spider on the window pane. It was on the move across the open expanse of glass – very surprising in a spider. They don't walk across open expanses of vertical glass as a rule. I went up to have a closer look.

It wasn't a spider at all, but a beetle: a weevil, to be precise, bottle-shaped and blackish-grey. It turned out to be *Otiorhyncus clavipes*, of the family Curculionidae. He's a plant feeder (says Michael Chinery), so I needn't kill him for being in the library. There are over 500 British Curculionidae (who classified them? Good luck to him!), all with well-marked rostra (beaks or snouts) and clubbed antennae, which are usually elbowed. I suppose yesterday's sunshine brought this chap out from hibernation, and then he popped into the library when it got a bit colder. Several of the Curculionidae are pretty colours – red or green. *Otiorhyncus clavipes*, however, is *not* attractive – he looks like a black-beetle, and moves sluggishly.

The sea very blue and still this morning, in warm sunshine, and the Mountains of Mourne plain among cumulus clouds.

17TH FEBRUARY

This afternoon I saw a stonechat along the cliff-top north of Peel. This is a bird I knew nothing of as a boy, living inland. I saw stonechats for the first time when I came to live here, where they are common enough along the cliffs. What puzzles me is that although they are mostly maritime they appear to get nothing from the sea and don't frequent the shore. They like open, furzy cliff-tops. This chap's head was blacker than one would expect at this time of year. They're usually sort of buff-black in winter and then go clear black as spring advances. Whatever they perch on, e.g. a gorse-bush or clump of bracken, they always sit on the very topmost point. They're attractive birds – so alert and energetic. It cheers you up just to see a cocky little stonechat bobbing and flitting about.

Later, an elderly and rather bedraggled pied wagtail ran very cheerfully within four feet of me, on the pavement along Peel front, even though I had Tetter with me on the lead.

> 'Soul clap its hands and sing, and louder sing
> For every tatter in its mortal dress.'

18TH FEBRUARY

Lichens are difficult. In Glen Helen I picked up a larch branch about three feet long, covered with at least three different kinds of lichen. They're not easy to identify from the coloured pictures in Brightman and Nicholson, good as the book is. One – an ordinary grey lichen – is, I'm fairly sure, *Hypogymnia physodes*, the commonest. There's some *Parmelia perlata* along with it. But most attractive to me are the long tufts of grey-green cotton wool (like miniature Spanish moss from Florida) called *Ramalina farinacea*. Then there are all sorts of 'flat', powdery lichens, like *Pertusaria amara*, and even green dust, like *Pleurococcus vulgaris*. A pity they haven't got common names: then people would notice them more.

19TH TO 22ND FEBRUARY

What on earth can you see in horrible London? I came to London, perforce, on Tuesday; now it's Friday. Well, some yellow crocuses blooming in Russell Square – like buttons, not yet fully out. And then the lilac bushes are beginning to show green. I've also seen one or two early blossoms of forsythia on otherwise bare bushes. Looking out of the hotel bedroom window at a waste patch of concrete and weeds below, I can see the big, palmate leaves of a plant of mallow among the dead kexes, and sticking up out of it last year's six-foot spike of dead bloom, tall as a hollyhock. Blackbirds sound nice singing between buildings, but not as nice as among trees in a garden.

23RD FEBRUARY

All day at an R.S.P.C.A. meeting in London. They showed a film called *Down on the Factory Farm*. Horrible. Most evil practices. Luke XVII, 2, I would think, for those fellows.

Beautiful crocuses in St James's Park – purple, gold; and striped. What Walter de la Mare called 'grey'? I always wondered what he meant.

> 'Light fails; night falls; the wintry moon
> Glitters; the crocus soon
> Will open grey and distracted
> On earth's austerity.'

In the park, as we went by, I caught sight of the pelicans on the lake. How well I remember them from civil service days! How glad I am to be going back to a home in the country! Timmy Willie's got nothing on me.

24TH FEBRUARY (*1st Sunday in Lent*)

'Almighty God, who hatest nothing that Thou hast made . . .' I should think not, on such a morning as this. The sun shining, a light mist covering the sea, a blackbird singing in the silence and the verges and banks covered with the dark-green, glossy burgeoning of Alexanders (*Smyrnium olusatrum*). The Island could be said to be *infested* with Alexanders. I'd never seen them until I came here, for they inhabit 'hedge-banks and waste ground near the sea' (Fitter, Fitter and Blamey). Like a lot of things uncommon in some areas, they're rampant in others. Two other plants we have in gross abundance: wild garlic and wall pennywort. In spring our woods actually reek of garlic.

wall pennywort

25TH FEBRUARY

The pair of pheasants are busily engaged in courtship, the cock following the hen up and down and round and round. With any luck they'll nest and produce a brood on my land.

I'm beginning to wish I hadn't seen that film about the factory farm. The chickens being de-beaked with a red-hot guillotine is something I'm not going to get out of my mind. Or the smug, clean gentleman in his white coat, talking about 'happy hens'. Does he believe it himself? It's like Dr Harry Rowsell's lies about the Canadian seals – you just say that black *is* white; and a lot of people swallow it because they don't want to take on board what it means to accept the truth; then they won't have to do anything.

On the factory farms, the film said, the lights are low or else out most of the time, because the animals are less aggressive so, and therefore damage themselves and each other less. Their misery passes in darkness or near-darkness.

26TH FEBRUARY

Out walking this afternoon I met Mr Faulds, a neighbour, at the door of his house above Gob-ny-Deigan. I inquired after his dog – a large, brown, smooth-haired youngster with a lot of energy. 'He got at the 'fridge,' replied Faulds feelingly, 'when no one was about, and he's just consumed £6 worth of meat.' While walking on, I observed the said dog tied up in the door of a barn. He looked replete, I thought.

Quiz – Whose dogs were: Diamond, Keeper, Flush, Dash, Wessex, Nigger, Brownie? (*Answers over page*)

27TH FEBRUARY

Another pretty fern: *Asplenium marinum*, the sea spleenwort, seen in a wall crevice three-quarters of a mile from the sea. The whole island's maritime, in effect. I dare say *Asplenium* grows at Injebreck (centre of the Island), come to that. It's a very miniature affair, dry and wiry, lying flat to the wall.

28TH FEBRUARY

asplenium marinum –

It's beginning to be a pleasure to be out of doors. No more slogging up muddy fields of mangel-wurzels in the dark! Tetter and I went out at 5 o'clock this evening in broad daylight and got back in twilight at 6.45. Saw: ribes in bloom (well, a bloom or two) and the barren strawberry (*Potentilla sterilis*) also in bloom, along the ditch below East Lhergy Dhoo Farm. The book says: 'Found in dry grassland and open woods', but this plant is on a distinctly wet bank with a runlet along the ditch below it. The book also says 'southern'. We're hardly that!

29TH FEBRUARY

barren strawberry

Mars is overtaking Jupiter. A week or two ago it was level with Jupiter and behind it. Now it's above it, so I suppose soon it will be ahead of it. Mars takes 1·881 years to go round the sun, and Jupiter takes 11·862 years. That's 6·3 times as long. But it's only about 3 times as far away from the sun. Which moves faster, I wonder? My book calls both planets 'slow-moving'. If I had a circle-describing compass I could calculate it by means of a diagram. How much greater is the circumference of a circle R3 than that of a circle R? Not 6 times greater, I would guess; more like 3 times. I have a notion that the further a planet is from the sun, the slower it moves. E.g. Mercury, 30 miles a second; Earth, 18·5; Pluto, 3. Must check this. (*Later*: it's correct. So Jupiter moves at less than half the speed of Mars.)

March

1ST MARCH (*Saturday*)

A little while ago (18th February) Elizabeth gave me a yellow polyanthus in a pot. It was covered with bloom. After about eight days in the library it was wilting and clearly in a bad way. I knocked it out of the pot and planted it in the garden. To-day I noticed that not only is it doing well, but the very blooms that were wilting have revived. What didn't it like in the library? There are no draughts. Sometimes the heating is boosted with one of those portable liquid gas heaters. But the potted cerise primrose on Janice's table has been doing fine for a fortnight, the hyacinths did very well and the Japanese miniature elm is happy. If there is gas in the air, *they* don't seem to mind it. Perhaps the polyanthus just didn't like its pot.

2ND MARCH

What a wonderful thing a timely jest is, to overcome embarrassment and reconcile people to something they might otherwise have taken amiss! A perfect example this morning on Radio 3. They played a recording of Beethoven's Pastoral Symphony. At the end the announcer said: 'I'm sorry that on that recording we seemed to have acquired not only a cuckoo and a quail, but also, at one point, a woodpecker.' Why don't I ever think of things like that?

In a cottage garden this afternoon, up in the north of the Island: the first daffodils I've seen in bloom, winter jasmine (*not* forsythia), scyllas, white aubretia, hellebore (both dark-red and white) and (wait for it!) purple stock – two blooms! A beautiful sunny afternoon. Nothing along the beach except gulls, ringed plovers and oyster-catchers.

3RD MARCH

Another beautiful day; sunshine and no wind. (I hate walking in the wind. I'd rather walk in the rain.) The sun, its bright circumference indistinct in a blue, brilliant haze, reminded me of the passage in Malory about the magical stone which came floating down the river to Camelot (Book XIII). 'The queen heard thereof . . . and shewed them the stone where it hoved on the water.' The sun looked like a heavy sphere borne up, rolling, dipping but not submerged in a fluid sky. ('Hove', I observe, is the original form of the modern word 'hover'.)

Elizabeth says that in Manchester, over the week-end, she saw coltsfoot in bloom. I've seen none yet; but I saw a few celandines to-day.

I watched, from the top of the cliff, a cormorant fishing in the sea below. (The Manx call them 'jinny-divers'.) On each of several dives it remained under for about forty seconds, and travelled, in my estimation, about sixty yards.

Nice to be out without a coat (only a scarf) and light, felt boots!

4TH MARCH

The weather has taken a turn for the worse. Grey and overcast all day, with a troublesome wind. I walked up sheltered Glen Helen. At the top, where the little river Rhenass joins the equally little river Blaber to form the Neb, there is a pretty cascade (of the Rhenass) about fourteen feet high, into a rock pool. Level with the lip of the fall, on the left, is a smooth, regular, hemi-spherical concavity in the rock, perhaps six feet in diameter. This, millions of years ago, must have been the original pool. The water broke through it and left it empty (when?). Below that is a second basin, similarly empty, and below that the present one. I wish I knew some geology.

The Rhenas Falls

5TH MARCH

A driving, heavy rain all day until tea-time: but at sunset there was such a display by the rooks as I've never seen in my life. There must have been thousands. The sky was half-covered. Sometimes the huge flock broke in different directions, so that the sky itself seemed falling apart. Then another lot, already settled among the pines of the Lhergy Dhoo, would start up and take wing again like a thick, flapping cloud of dark smoke in the twilight, opening out as they rose higher. The incessant cawing was all around, filling the air; an urgent, aggressive sound. The birds were not sailing placidly, as on a fine summer evening. Their flight was rapid, with no gliding. Elizabeth and I watched entranced for about twenty minutes, from the little balcony outside the kitchen door. It seemed to be snowing rooks.

A song-thrush sang most beautifully in the last light. They like a wet March evening.

6TH MARCH

Rain or no rain, I had to get out a bit, so I had Janice drop me at Ballig about quarter to five. Thrushes bawling and wrens trilling in the hedges. In a garden near Tynwald Mills I saw a shrub new to me, though I dare say it's well known to many. Its new, unfurling leaves, small and pointed, were a pretty, fairly deep pink; but the older leaves had turned green: the growth very regular all over the shrub.

7TH MARCH

Up betimes, and to the airport, and so to Heathrow. Elizabeth, Janice and I took the hired car to Hampton Court, Janice never having been there before. The prunus and almond trees were in bloom along the suburban roads. I love to see prunus bloom on the leafless tree. The tiny, pale flowers look like a drift of snowflakes. (What I loosely call 'prunus' is, of course, *Prunus pissardii* 'Atropurpurea', the earliest common prunus to come into flower. Almond is *Prunus dulcis* or *Prunus communis*.) Prunus does better in the suburbs, very often, than in the country, since the bullfinches don't get at the buds.

Hampton Court was half-closed for the winter. Mistletoe

the Long Water / Hampton Court

growing very high on the still-bare trees by the Long Water. The weather bright but cold, with intermittent squally showers.

8TH MARCH

I spoke at the annual demonstration against the harp seal slaughter. I reminded the audience that it had taken about thirty-five years' campaigning to abolish corporal punishment in the army and navy, and about thirty years' ditto to abolish the slave trade. I probably shan't live to see the abolition of the slaughter, but some of those present to-day will. The Canadian Government are running very scared, in my view. They are resorting to personal defamation of individuals (e.g. of Bill Jordan, senior wildlife officer of the R.S.P.C.A.). What a wicked, evil institution is this slaughter! I feel like Laertes – 'Do you see this, O God?'

Returning to Heathrow, I saw a kestrel perching on the horizontal top of a tall, thin, inward-projecting lamp standard beside the motorway. It improved the lamp standard no end.

9TH MARCH (*Sunday*)

Bright, rather cold weather. In the afternoon Stewart and I walked from Kirk Michael to Orrisdale, returning first along the top of the sandy cliffs and then descending to the beach. In a thicket beside the disused railway line we heard a greenfinch (*cheeeeee, cheeeeee*) and also a hedge-sparrow singing very sweetly in a bush, almost at my elbow.

37

Along the cliffs, we unexpectedly recognized fulmars below us, and stopped for some little time to watch them on the wing. I've never been so closely approached by fulmars before. Two or three repeatedly flew past within a few feet of us. They seem able to glide (and soar) almost indefinitely, without beating their wings at all. These beat their wings only to slow down or check in the air before sweeping away on a fresh course. The white face and dark, 'mascara' eye-patch are very beautiful. Double tubular nostrils in the beak very noticeable.

10TH MARCH

The dwarf cyclamen by the cascade are now in full bloom and look charming; one clump pink, the other dark red. I must also bestow a passing pat on the back to that honest saxifrage, the pink bergenia. I've always thought this a rather dull plant, but it can be relied upon to display thick clusters of bloom at this early time of year. Ours is doing just that, in a border still waiting for most of its plants even to look like blooming.

IITH MARCH

Along the waste land just above the shore, down by White Strand, I found the coltsfoot (*Tussilago farfara*) in bloom – two or three blooms. The first dandelion-type Composita of the spring. Good!

Daffodils now blooming everywhere. Snowdrops are virtually over, but still plenty of crocuses.

coltsfoot

12TH MARCH

Outside the kitchen window we have two magnificent trees; one an ash, the other a wych-elm. The wych-elm is now in flower; pretty, deep-red flowers on the bare tree. The flowers, says Alan Mitchell, are 'perfect', i.e. with the organs of both sexes in the one flower.

Tetter and I out for a walk in April-like weather – sun and intermittent showers, a bit cold. Down by the Neb, near Tynwald Mills, I heard the trilled song of a tit in a nearby tree – *te-wissaker wissaker wissaker*. I looked up and saw a great tit. This seemed odd, for I could have sworn that what I had heard was a blue tit. A few moments later the blue tit obligingly appeared and sang again, as though to corroborate me, before flying across to a nut-bag hung up in a cottage garden.

Saw shepherd's purse and groundsel in bloom.

13TH MARCH

I found a good, thick patch of golden saxifrage (*Chrysoplenium oppositifolium*) in bloom down by the Neb near Tynwald Mills. It likes a shaded, wet bank. The odd thing is that although the unpetalled flowers are tiny – just eight minute anthers in an irregular circle not a great deal bigger than a pin-head – they show up very 'golden' from a little distance. The bigger leaves are lightly bristly right across the face.

Shepherd's purse

14TH MARCH

Clif Dadd showed up this morning to reconnoitre the future lake, and I asked him to identify the pink-leaved shrub (6th March). It's a *Spiraea*; *japonica*, he thinks, but will confirm. The pretty, secluded back lanes down along the Neb were unknown to Clif, so I took him to see my favourite cottage garden (1st January) where we saw some lungwort (*Pulmonaria*) blooming red and blue, and two bushes of *Skimmia japonica*, male and female on opposite sides of the garden path, coming along nicely. Both the hydrangea, and the rambler rose on the pergola at the gate, had been pruned all ready for summer, and the vegetable patch was freshly dug. Two rows of leeks still left. All in all, an encouraging and refreshing sight.

15TH MARCH

Missel-thrush singing beautifully this morning under the Lhergy Dhoo. A goldcrest working along the hawthorns this afternoon, too. Goodness, how tiny!

Missel-thrush? Mistle-thrush? Missle-thrush? Why, anyway? Apparently from its fondness for the berries of the mistletoe (Old High German, 'mistil'). But *Viscum album* is mistletoe ('white berry') and hence Linnaeus called the bird *Turdus viscivorus*. *The Shorter O.E.D.* prefers 'missel-thrush', but then it has 'mistletoe'. So it's all accordin', as they say in Berkshire.

16TH MARCH (*Sunday*)

The clocks went forward last night, but if this is the first day of summer you can keep it. Bleak, bitterly cold though not freezing, overcast and dull. I observe that the weeping willow (*Salix alba tristis*), opposite the northern kitchen window, is well on in leaf.

Patrick Moore, consulted on the telephone, advises a six-inch reflector telescope from Mr Fuller in the Farringdon Road. I shall go and see Mr F. personally. Can't just order a six-inch telescope on the nod. Will need to learn how to hold, aim and fire.

17TH MARCH

Snow this morning! Not much, but it's lying on Snaefell and the other tops. The Greeba Ridge looks its best under snow, I think: a gleaming, white expanse extending above St John's, peaceful, smooth and remote. Slieau Whallian, being largely wooded on the St John's side, can't make the same effect. Brave little robins singing in the hedgerows, but nothing else singing, of course.

18TH MARCH

Some of the snow is gone, but it's still lying on the tops. These last few days have been like playing out a maiden over. The diarist can do little while he can't score off Nature's bowling. The year is not progressing during these bleak days. 'Rien de nouveau,' as Louis XVI remarked.

This morning came news from the R.S.P.C.A that Granada T.V. at Manchester want Bill Jordan, the Society's senior wildlife officer, and me to appear to-morrow afternoon to talk about the Newfoundland harp seal slaughter. Apparently they have got a Newfoundland M.P., one Carter, who happens to be over here, to 'confront' us. To-day's Daily Express gives both full front-page and centre-page 'spread' coverage to the slaughter, attacking it strongly. Dare one hope that public opinion in this country may at last rise up and demand that imports be banned?

Bill Jordan arrived on the evening flight. How glad I am to see him!

19TH MARCH

Bill, Janice and I flew to Manchester. I am impressed with Granada T.V. The young compère, by name Nick Turnbull, was, I thought, excellent. Carter was clearly nervous – kept a low profile, and didn't put up any real case. The audience voted overwhelmingly against the seal slaughter. Afterwards I (politely) refused to talk to Mr Carter backstage (he tried to talk to me) because he is supporting

Greeba under Snow –

an evil, cruel, vile activity – a horrible abuse of wildlife. How could we converse? I replied, 'Mr Carter, I won't be *rude* to you,' and said no more.

20TH MARCH

Bill left this afternoon. The weather still bleak, but it came out a fine evening, so although I'd done five miles with Bill in the morning, I did another five with Tetter. Blue tits, greenfinches, curlews, plus the aforesaid missel-thrush in splendid voice.

I observe that the stinging nettles are coming up nicely along the hedgerows. The young plant has a pretty shape, the new leaves, almost circular, forming a kind of rosette close to the ground.

Apparently Granada have told the R.S.P.C.A. that our programme yesterday was very good and the public reaction excellent.

21ST MARCH

Woke to a blizzard this morning – two inches of snow already. Nevertheless, I was able to get the car up the drive. (It's steep and sometimes, in snow, you can't.) Janice 'phoned to report traffic chaos in Douglas – she daren't come.

Working, I watched the snow showers approaching across the choppy Irish Sea – tall, swirling pillars of half-darkness, apocalyptic. Rintra roars and shakes his fires in the burdened air. Hungry clouds swag on the deep.

22ND MARCH (*Saturday*)

Some of the snow gone to-day, but not on the tops; it's still very cold. But it was so bright and clear that I determined on a good, long walk. Elizabeth dropped me and Tetter at Round Table, under South Barrule. Children and their parents were tobogganing on the thin snow. I climbed South Barrule, then went across by the Old Mines and Dearlish Ard and so up and over Slieau Whallian. A cold wind, but mercifully it was behind me. The new gorse very bright. Then down the broogh to Ballaspit and St John's, and back home along the disused railway line. It took three hours and forty minutes and I suppose it might be a shade over nine miles. Saw rooks, carrion crows, jackdaws, hooded crows. (No ravens; no choughs.)

Tetter now learning to walk to heel, as he's getting on for a year old. So far he's doing well. He's a very good dog – anxious to do what you want, as long as he can grasp what that is.

24TH MARCH

Awake this morning at six, I was lying in bed listening to the birds. The missel-thrush was going great guns and every now and then the cock pheasant went off like another. A great tit was ringing away for dear life. Evidently a thaw. Then I heard what sounded like the sustained, sweet song of some small bird, like a warbler. What could it possibly be? My own chest was wheezing away like Mr Jogglebury Crowdey (or Mr Sponge) and this increased my perplexity, for I couldn't hear distinctly. At last I felt so much baffled that I got up and went to the window in the half-light. I couldn't *see* my quarry, but I could hear – *and* distinguish! A robin and a wren were singing simultaneously – very pretty, the phrases and trills combining. All the same, it strikes me that wrens don't often sit and sing on and on, like thrushes or blackbirds. They usually sing once or twice as they're going about their business, and then pause for a bit. This one was singing pretty steadily; hence my confusion.

A fine, warm afternoon. Walking down by the Neb, saw the first wood anemones (*Anemone nemorosa*) in bloom. I've always loved these exquisitely beautiful, scentless, white flowers; frail,

delicate frequenters of woods and shady banks. I never pick them, for they wither in ten minutes. I also noticed that along the stone walls the English stonecrop (*Sedum anglicum*), very common here, is already well into this year's new growth.

25TH MARCH — *Tetter in Glen Helen*

What ho for celandines! All along the banks they're blooming! I don't know why celandines have never had the same popularity as primroses and violets. They don't smell, it's true, but there's the beautiful star-shape, and the attractive way the petals turn white as the bloom begins to fade. The eight petals (good value!) are glossy gold, too. They deserve to be more fully associated with romance, like violets.

> Accept, dear sweetheart, mistress mine,
> This bunch of shining celandine.
> Each flower, radiant like a star,
> An emblem is how fair you are.

Is this a prologue or the posy of a ring?

26TH MARCH

'Across' again this afternoon, to London via Liverpool, to meet Richard Ryder and several other R.S.P.C.A. Council members for a discussion on policy.

I noticed, while walking to the Canonbury flat, that in the urban gardens there seem to be a great many of those funny little, pale-yellow crocuses. They must be becoming popular. Can't think why.

44

27TH MARCH

Following up Patrick Moore's advice (16th March), bought an eight-and-a-half-inch telescope at Mr Fuller's in the Farringdon Road. It won't arrive till August. Also bought a copy of Patrick's *The Amateur Astronomer*. Very good stuff, though he sometimes omits to define his terms. What, for instance, is 'escape velocity'?

Flew back this afternoon. Pouring with rain.

28TH MARCH

In this continuing bleak snap, the year is not going forward. However, I did notice one or two engaging things this afternoon. Here, we rejoice in plenty of the little, creeping, prickly, cream-coloured wild roses called *Rosa pimpinellifolia* – the burnet rose. ('On sand dunes, cliffs and heaths, mostly near the sea.') In the lane below East Lhergy Dhoo Farm I noticed several leaves already out, along the edge of the ditch. At first glance I mistook them for meadow-sweet. In the shady, sylvan garden of 'Langtoft', an isolated house further down the lane, the dwarf red-and-yellow tulips were well on in bud: indeed, on the point of flowering.

The brook that runs into the sea at the south end of White Strand was in heavy spate, turgid and sandy-brown. It had coloured the sea to a distance of about three hundred yards off-shore. This discoloration stopped along an irregular but quite distinct line –

brown one side, blue the other – which revealed that the muddy, fresh water, having entered the sea across the beach, fanned out for a little distance but then 'set' northward, only becoming indistinguishable from the rest of the sea perhaps four hundred yards north of the outfall. This general line of flow appeared as clearly as if the sandy-brown colour had been laid on over the blue with a huge paint-brush.

29TH MARCH

A delightful walk with Stewart (and Tetter) along the cliffs at Santon – that is, the centre (more or less) of the south coast of the Island. Noticed grape hyacinths and a bed of startlingly beautiful, blue *Anemone blanda* in a cottage garden.

Along the cliff footpath, we encountered the eccentric but fundamentally amiable Mr Kinrade. Mr Kinrade, who owns all the land around there, looks rather as I imagine Cecil Sharp's folk singer Shepherd Haden. He has a long, grey beard, and was wearing an ex-W.D. jungle hat and an old, nondescript coat. He began, in minatory vein, 'And where are *you* gentlemen going?' but became quite genial after a chat. I demonstrated Tetter's perfect obedience, which I think impressed him; but he nevertheless pointed out that pregnant ewes will run even from a distant dog on a lead. True. (I should explain here that on the Isle of Man O.S. map, no footpaths are shown in red as public rights of way. Some paths have in fact been established by the Public Rights of Way Tribunal, but one does not always know which these are. Landowners, however, are friendly for the most part. I have never had any unpleasantness with a landowner.)

30TH MARCH (*Palm Sunday*)

I found an early scurvy-grass (*Cochlearia danica*) in full bloom; and nothing so very remarkable about that, I dare say, for Fitter, Fitter and Blamey give the blooming period as January onward. Nevertheless, it was the first I've come across. Also, along the Poortown road, a nice little hairy bittercress (*Cardamine hirsuta*). I don't despise it. Lots of people lump the small white Cruciferae together as 'chickweed', but in fact they differ a lot. Hairy bittercress: 'A compact rosette of pinnate leaves. Flowers less obvious than long, erect pods.'

April

1ST APRIL

Saw mauve, spherical-headed *Primula denticulata* in bloom in 'Langtoft' garden; also purple violas.

The elder bushes are in leaf, and about time too!

2ND APRIL

The sun is setting noticeably further to the north. The Mountains of Mourne were very clear this evening, behind a bright, Claude Lorrain-like sea.

3RD APRIL (*Maundy Thursday*)

A beautiful day; the first of summer, I hope. But still no chiff-chaff. Saw several grouse on the high ground. When you put them up, they gain speed with quick wing-beats, then glide away on outspread, downward-curving wings, as partridges do.

Several little trout, about six-ouncers, rising to the fly (what fly? I couldn't even see it) in the clear water of the upper Neb in Glen Helen. The laurel is budding in finger-like, greenish-white spikes.

Tony Kellett, my architect, dropped in this morning and explained, inter alia, about 'escape velocity' (27th March). Apparently it means the speed at which something has to be going

47

before it can get out of the gravitational pull of another celestial body. In other words, a back-handed way of referring to the gravitational power of a planet, moon, etc.

4TH APRIL (*Good Friday*)

Juliet (my elder daughter) and her husband Peter arrived for the Easter holiday.

This has been the warmest, sunniest day so far this year. In fact, summer is here (but no chiff-chaff). Julie, Peter and I walked from Peel to Glenmaye in perfect weather. The gorse smelt lovely. Saw a raven along the cliff-top. In Glenmaye itself the rooks were building, and I saw pink wood-sorrel (*Oxalis acetosella*) in bloom – first this year.

5TH APRIL

Last night was perfect for star observation; very clear and fine, and no moon. At half-past ten four planets were to be seen – Venus, Mars, Jupiter and Saturn. Venus at half-phase, close to the Pleiades, was a notable sight. The other three were all in Leo.

Another fine day. About seven o'clock this evening, returning from a walk along the Switchback, I saw a spotted flycatcher hunting from a thorn tree. The Collins *Pocket Guide* reckons they arrive about 10th April. If it wasn't a spotted flycatcher I don't know what it was. The behaviour is hard to mistake.

Yellowhammers singing in the early-flowering gorse.

6TH APRIL (*Easter Sunday*)

A perfect Easter morning. Francis Kilvert would have been moved to one of his ecstatic rhapsodies. I arrived at Ballaugh Old Church a few minutes before 8.30 a.m. and walked across the churchyard full of daffodils to greet Roger Greenhouse, one of the church-wardens, pulling the bell-rope outside the west door.

In the afternoon, walked up through the Ravensdale woods to Druidale, round and back; after that, up Glen Mooar to Spooyt Vane and so round by the lane; after that, up Glen Helen to the Keeill and back. No bird-song to speak of. Found common speedwell (*Veronica persica*) just coming into bloom. Also hairy bittercress (*Cardamine hirsuta*) and the common chickweed (*Stellaria media*).

Ballaugh old Church –

The patches of willow-bloom below the house are now fully out, a soft golden colour, continually moving in the wind.

Venus, still glittering away like mad, has now reached its greatest elongation.

8TH APRIL

What an extraordinary variety of calls and sounds the curlew has! As well as the bubbling, rising, repetitive cry which every dweller in the north knows, it seems to be able to make virtually any whistling noise. Lying in bed this morning at about half-past six, I really thought I could hear humans whistling two- or three-note phrases outside. Smugglers? Poachers? No – curlews!

Our curlews feed on the beaches at low tide; then fly back to the fields and moors as dusk falls. What *enormously* long beaks – they strike you afresh each time you see them! They're as long as the whole of the rest of the bird, or nearly. Evolved over millions of years, presumably, for poking about both in deep heather and in rock-pools.

9TH APRIL

Venus is now going away from the Pleiades – upwards! Mars is returning towards Jupiter – backwards! Or, to quote the *Times* chap, it's 'reversing its motion from retrograde to direct'.

The horse chestnut is covered with sticky buds. The *Populus candicans*, or scented poplar, is in early leaf and beautifully fragrant.

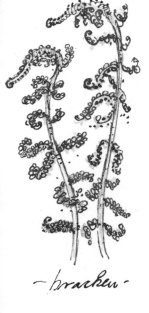

10TH APRIL

A smell of new-mown grass and a wood-pigeon cooing down by the Neb. Also a smell of box, for the weather is much warmer. Box needs sun to bring out its scent. Saw a fresh, new plant of red campion in bloom, very different from the washed-out winter left-overs. Also the first greater stitchwort (*Stellaria holostea*) just coming out. Two or three fronds of new bracken, each about six inches high, curled like a bishop's crozier and sandy in colour.

11TH APRIL

Plenty of vetch and goose-grass coming up in the hedgerows.

50

– bracken –

In Glen Helen this afternoon I saw a pair of grey wagtails (*Motacilla cinerea*) working over the smooth, half-dry rocks of the bed of a steep cascade. The clear yellow under-plumage was very conspicuous, as was the long, slim, dark tail, which never stops going up and down (what a lot of energy it must need!) but with a smoother, less jerky, more graceful movement than that of the pied wagtail. That pair will almost certainly build in Glen Helen. Grey wagtails need a crevice or cavity to nest. There are plenty in the rocks surrounding the steep waterfalls up and down the glen.

12TH APRIL

Elizabeth was up before me this morning and, going out with Tetter into the garden, heard the chiff-chaff. One up to her!

In the afternoon, a rather arduous walk with Stewart over the high moor west of Snaefell. Scrambling up out of a peat-hag, we came upon a wheatear (*Oenanthe oenanthe*) bobbing about within a few feet of our eyes. It was a male in spring plumage; black, grey, white and ochre, very smart. Off he went, white rump flashing above the grey, unsprouted heather. I've never been so close to one before: they're rather shy birds. We also saw two ravens, a lot of grouse, a kestrel and a skylark or two.

The bilberries, I notice, are beginning to put forth leaves along their tough, rather wiry green stems.

The leaves of the bonsai elm are coming out in great style – a pretty sight.

~ grey wagtails -

13TH APRIL

Saw what was either a swallow or a house martin fly past the library windows this afternoon. It was going rather fast and what attracted my attention, almost too late, was the characteristic flight-behaviour. But a Hirundinida it certainly was.

14TH APRIL

One of the glories of the Island is its extensive banks of wild violets. In England, people tend to get quite excited if they find wild violets. Here they're common. At this time of year the roadside

the bonsai elm -

banks are inlaid with them – beautiful, glowing areas of colour, often mingled with thick clumps of primroses. This, of course, is the unscented dog violet (*Viola riviniana*), in Somerset called 'blue mice'. The lowest, central petal of the five in each bloom is larger than the other four, and delicately striped black and white at the base.

Also saw: some early blooms of cow-parsley (*Anthriscus sylvestris*, I think, but there are so many kinds), sheltered from the cutting wind between two stout brick pillars of a disused gate. Red dead-nettle (*Lamium purpureum*). A nice patch of forget-me-not (*Myosotis scorpioides*) along a ditch beside the Poortown road. (I suppose it could have been *Myosotis sylvatica*: must check this.) And honesty (*Lunaria rediviva*) blooming in 'Langtoft' garden.

Tetter's heel-work is now very fair indeed.

anthriscus —

— myosotis

15TH APRIL

Heard a willow warbler (*Phylloscopus trochilus*) in the scrub willow this morning. The characteristic dying fall is unmistakable, though I think Dr Burton is going a bit far in describing it as 'a sparkling, descendant cascade of notes'. I find it a quiet, rather melancholy little song. It was Gilbert White, God rest his soul, who first distinguished the willow warbler from the chiff-chaff.

A gloriously soft, warm, sunny day. Tetter and I did about six miles. The gorse is coming into blaze everywhere. Close up, it fairly bids the rash gazer wipe his eye: you can hardly look steadily at the brilliant, deep gold, like a swarm of miraculous bees. Does *anything* smell nicer than gorse? (Yes: wistaria; azalea; jasmine.) Well, but any *wild* flower? (Yes: *Petasites fragrans*; lily of the valley; soapwort; cowslips; meadow-sweet.) I *still* like gorse!

Diary, this is what we joined up for! The red blood reigns in the winter's pale!

16TH APRIL

Up at six o'clock and by 'plane to Manchester, where I was met and driven to Hull for a couple of speaking engagements, one in the afternoon and one in the evening.

My host's garden reminded me of Wemmick's in *Great Expectations*, for it was hardly bigger than a cricket pitch (a back garden to a terrace house). Yet it contained a pool (with toads and goldfish), a fine apple tree coming into bloom, a *Clematis montana rubens* in bud along the fence, a beautiful group of six or seven golden crown imperials in bloom, and several auriculas, both purple and maroon, blooming in a wooden tub. There was much else in that garden, e.g. well-pruned roses, and peonies shooting nicely. What a treat to see a town garden full of thriving plants (and creatures) which someone really loves and looks after!

17TH APRIL

After breakfast, saw a queen wasp cruising speculatively along the ivy-clad wall of the hotel. No doubt, like the boll weevil, a-lookin' fer a home. Didn't interfere.

Came by train from Hull to Manchester. As the train passed at moderate speed through a cutting, I saw a fox sitting at the mouth of an earth, only a few yards away, calmly watching the train go by.

On the way home from Ronaldsway (the Isle of Man airport), stopped to check on the forget-me-not (14th April). It's plainly a garden escape; plants big, growth rampant, blooms quite large. *Myosotis sylvatica*, I'm now sure. Heard the chiff-chaff myself – and about blithering time, too!

18TH APRIL

This afternoon, up on the moor above Sky Hill, I watched and listened to the skylarks for a time. I remembered how odd it was, in America, to be teaching Spenser, Shelley and Milton's 'Lycidas' to sizeable groups of young people, not one of whom had ever heard a skylark or had the faintest idea of its song or flight-behaviour.

I watched one lark come down, after a song-flight, quite near me, and remain *couchant* for some time on top of a tussock of heather. It was half-concealed, inconspicuous and passive. As I cautiously approached, it sat up alertly on its heather-cushion, crest erect and speckled breast very prominent. Alert, it no longer looked timorous but quite self-assertive.

19TH APRIL

It's blowing hard this morning, with the sea covered in white horses; but the sun is shining brightly. The wind doesn't deter the willow warbler from singing.

The relative paucity of Sylviidae (warblers) in the Island I have always felt as a bit of a deprivation. Willow warblers are plentiful enough, and sing right on into October. The chiff-chaff, too, is common. But blackcaps mostly seem to drop in and then move on. You'll hear one, in May, in a particular spot, but after a few days he's usually gone. I wonder whither? Nor have I ever heard a garden warbler on the Island. Whitethroats we get, but I can't recall hearing a wood warbler.

I note, from *Birds of the Isle of Man* (pub. Manx Museum and National Trust), that, officially, the following are all regular summer visitors and breed: grasshopper warbler, sedge warbler, blackcap, garden warbler (!), whitethroat, willow warbler, chiff-chaff. The following drop in on passage: barred warbler (autumn), lesser whitethroat (scarce passage migrant), wood warbler (regular on spring and autumn passage). Well, you could have fooled me.

20TH APRIL

Still squally and blustery. Went down to the ford near Cashtal yn Ard, on the east side of the Island, and did the little Port Cornaa to Ballaglass Glen walk. (Four and a half miles.) In the Isle of Man a maritime place called 'Port So-and-So' *may* be a port (e.g. Port Erin, Port St Mary) but as often as not it's only a sheltered cove, no more. E.g. Port Grenaugh, Port Soderick, Port Cornaa.

Saw some beautiful, dark-red *Dicentra spectabilis* (bleeding hearts) in full bloom along the front of a cottage. In the woods, near the

at Port Cornaa-

stream that runs into the sea at Port Cornaa, found a great sheet of kingcups (marsh marigolds, *Caltha palustris*) in full bloom – about sixty yards of them. Kingcups affect me as the daffodils affected Wordsworth. But if it comes to description, I can't do better than Gerard, writing in 1597: 'Marsh Marigold hath great broad leaves, somewhat round, smooth, of a gallant greene colour, slightly indented or purlde about the edges, among which rise up thicke fat stalkes, likewise greene; where-upon do growe goodly yellow flowers, glittering like gold.'

A clear, starlit night with a waxing moon. Venus a little below Auriga in the west at 10.30 p.m.

Tetter nervous...

21ST APRIL

Walked from St John's to Peel along the disused railway line, then back along the cliffs. In the Neb valley, saw the first bluebells (*Endymion nonscriptus*) in bloom (*and* whitebells); a bank of lesser periwinkles (*Vinca minor*), red currant in bloom (*Ribes rubrum*), its little green flowers forming drooping spikes; and in the marsh, water horsetails coming on in great numbers (*Equisetum fluviatile*). Meadow-sweet plants leafing thickly. Willow warblers singing all down the valley. Blustery along the front at Peel. Tetter nervous of the breaking spray and ran from it.

22ND APRIL

From a tree in the hedgerow below East Lhergy Dhoo Farm I picked some white blossom resembling, yet visibly not, may. It turns out to be the bullace, or wild plum (*Prunus insititia*): the

white bloom rather showy, a little larger than blackthorn. There's an old superstition against bringing white blossom into a house. Never mind; it looks beautiful – white bloom and green leaves – on my desk.

23RD APRIL

Shakespeare's birthday! And a beautiful, warm, sunny day. Dr Johnson was fond of composing prayers for this occasion and that, so here goes, and very sincerely.

'Almighty God, in Whom the Word was made flesh, and who hast conferred upon Thy human creatures Thy most excellent gift of speech and language, we humbly thank Thee for the joy, wisdom and truth revealed, and especially to the English-speaking peoples, by Thy servant William Shakespeare. And grant, O Lord, that we, following his noble example, may always honour and respect the English tongue, feel and preserve its beauty and ourselves use it gracefully and rightly: through Jesus Christ our Lord. Amen.'

24TH APRIL

In a garden near Spooyt Vane to-day, I saw a fairly large clump of yellow fritillaries in bloom. The delicately shaped petals and characteristic, drooping heads were most striking.

Up on the moor, I came across *Cladonia bellidiflora*, a mountain lichen, fairly common on peaty soil in hilly areas. The little spikes of this lichen are greenish-grey, except for the tops, which consist of bright-red apothecia. The effect is of tiny red-hot pokers, clusters of little sticks with scarlet top-knots. In New England they're called 'British soldiers'. I told this to Clif Dadd, who replied that he'd been brought up to call them 'Devil's matchsticks'.

25TH APRIL

This morning, driving the car under the mountain called Sartfell, I saw a bird lying in the road. I stopped and picked it up. It was a cock linnet, the rosy breast very clear and beautiful. I could see no injury, but it seemed dazed. I brought it back to Knocksharry, whence it flew away over the gorse, apparently none the worse. The builder's men were interested, and asked me what it was as I released it.

26TH APRIL

In the old railway cutting I came upon a bush of broom (*Cytisus scoparius*), covered with buds, and two blooms just out. I also found ivy-leaved toadflax (*Cymbalaria muralis*) flowering on a wall, the new blooms very pretty on their long, thin stalks; and in a cliff-top pasture, the cut-leaved cranesbill (*Geranium dissectum*) in bloom.

There was a nuthatch (*Sitta europaea*) in the big ash tree below the library this afternoon. Might there be a pair, and might they breed?

I saw a red admiral at Orrisdale, and in Glen Wyllin the first common vetch in bloom (*Vicia sativa*); a beautiful, glowing purple.

On a sandy cliff-top meadow at Orrisdale, I found *Erodium cicutarium* variant *pimpinellifolium*; the common storksbill (a wild geranium). The two upper of the five petals have a dark spot, and this (with the help of the Rev. Keble Martin) is how I identified it. Near it was *Geranium molle*, the soft or dove's-foot cranesbill, with little, pale-pink flowers.

27TH APRIL

Great banks of primroses everywhere, thick. Violets all among them.

Rather cold and cloudy to-day. There's been so little rain that even the wettest spots (which I have come to know all too well) are dry, and walking is easy.

The bonsai elm is now in full leaf. It still seems very healthy.

In the evening, flew across to London.

29TH APRIL

Cherry trees, lilac and tulips in London make it full of colour. In St James's Park the apple blossom, small azaleas and rhododendrons are in bloom. The smell of apple blossom, cool and watery, always turns me over afresh each spring. As I sat writing at the window of the Canonbury flat this afternoon, looking out over the well-kept back gardens, a drake mallard flew down and alighted on the little pond of the garden next door but one. The blackbirds singing between the buildings brought to mind how glad I used to be to hear them, in London-imprisoned, civil service days. Plenty of blue tits in inner London nowadays, I observe. Clean air makes all the difference.

Returning to the Isle of Man, I noticed that the blackthorn is now in bloom everywhere; drifts of white against bare boughs in the hedgerows. The corn is up, too; all the formerly bare fields now green. The wild cherry grove at the southern end of the Switchback road is in bloom.

Elizabeth tells me she heard the cuckoo this afternoon. It arrives relatively late in the Island, of course.

view from the
Canonbury flat

To Edinburgh to-day, to address the Scottish Society for the Prevention of Vivisection, at their annual general meeting, about the Newfoundland harp seal slaughter.

On the outskirts of Edinburgh, I saw a weeping wych-elm. I don't think I've ever seen one before.

What everyone nowadays calls lady-smocks (*Cardamine pratensis*) were out along the motorway between Glasgow and Edinburgh.

> 'When daisies pied, and violets blue,
> And lady-smocks all silver-white:
> And cuckoo-buds of yellow hue,
> Do paint the meadows with delight . . .'

And what, pray, were Shakespeare's 'lady-smocks'? Not *Cardamine pratensis*. That's pale mauve. Dover Wilson suggests, very plausibly, that they were *stitchworts* (*Stellaria holostea*) – the whitest of all spring flowers. I'd go along with that. The shape of the bloom suggests a white, frilly petticoat. But Geoffrey Grigson (*The Englishman's Flora*) gives 'lady's smock' as a local name for the greater stitchwort only in Somerset and Cornwall. 'All silver-white' is apt, though, and the flower is abundant enough to make it appropriate to say that it 'paints the meadows'.

On 'cuckoo-buds of yellow hue' Dover Wilson is less certain. 'Unexplained; the marsh marigold, buttercup and cowslip have all been suggested.' Well, but the first doesn't 'paint the meadows': it likes only wet places. I think that out of that three, I'd back the cowslip. Shakespeare liked cowslips, I infer. (Mentioned in *Midsummer Night's Dream*, *Cymbeline* and *The Tempest*.)

On return, made a new cross-kern to put inside the front door. This is a cross made of rowan twigs bound together with sheep's wool. Its purpose is to deter malicious fairies and goblins. It has to be renewed each year on the night of 30th April–1st May. This custom remains common throughout the Island and no one laughs at it.

May

1ST MAY

The bonsai elm's leaves are grown much bigger than expected. The tree itself is just short of seven inches high, but the biggest leaves are a good one and a half inches long. Out of scale, really. Never mind; it looks healthy.

Tetter now walks to heel with virtually total reliability.

Saw a common bat (*Pipistrellus pipistrellus*) hunting round the house at twilight. The smallest British bat. (There are eighteen different sorts!)

2ND MAY

Moorhens don't necessarily need much water, it seems. Any wet area will do. A pair have lived for over a year in the willow brake along the edge of Roy Callin's field below this house. I'm expecting them to nest. The place gets quite dry in summer, but they don't leave. I see them pecking about among the rabbits in the evening. Neither the moorhens nor the rabbits seem to mind each other.

3RD MAY

An excellent walk with Stewart in the Port Cornaa vicinity. The kingcups (20th April) are still in full bloom.

Saw a cabbage white and an orange tip. (Butterflies.)

I picked up Venus in the field-glasses early this evening, just on sunset. One could see that it was a three-quarter disc, like a gibbous moon.

4TH MAY

The uplands of the Island could almost be said to be *infested* with hares. This is *Lepus timidus scoticus*, the Scottish or Variable hare. They are pretty creatures, compact and less leggy and lollopy than the brown hare of the south. Just now they're all turning back from white to brown, for the summer. They change from the head backwards, so at present we have hundreds of bi-coloured hares, brown in front and a rather grubby-looking, speckled white in rear. There are very few predators here, so they're abundant. Climbing the ridge of North Barrule from Corony vale, Stewart and I saw seven or eight along the slope and the ridge.

Mars now very close to Jupiter.

5TH MAY

Referring once more to the common vetch (26th April) I found more to-day and the blooms were of so intense and glowing a purple (or magenta?) that I wondered whether it might not be what the Rev. Keble Martin calls '*Vicia angustifolia*', the narrow-leaved vetch. Now the funny thing is that Fitter, Fitter and Blamey don't include anything called *Vicia angustifolia* at all. But my Hooker (published 1884) has it. Yet Fitch and Smith (*Illustrations of the British Flora*, 1946) hasn't. Meanwhile the blooms, intensely purple, care nothing for classification.

Along the half-bituminous, sandy pathway beside the Peel road I found a very insignificant little plant I didn't know, with tiny, almost invisible clusters of five-petalled blooms set in green tufts at the tops of the stalks. These minute flowers were nearly white, but to my eye included the faintest tinge of blue. I had to use a magnifying glass to see them clearly. I had a bit of a job to identify the plant, but it turns out to be annual knawel (*Scleranthus annuus*) – dry, sandy places; blooming May to October.

Again saw the nuthatch in the ash tree. (26th April.)

Surprised to see a bloom of red geum out already in the border: due, no doubt, to the prolonged warm, dry weather.

6TH MAY

Elizabeth, Janice and I flew to Copenhagen for a few days with Jarl Borgen, my Danish publisher. I enjoyed flying in over the flat Danish countryside, all fields and straight canals from above. It looked rather like Tenniel's picture of Alice's chess-board country-side in *Through the Looking-Glass*.

7TH MAY

In Copenhagen. Everything here is rather less advanced than in the Isle of Man, for we are on about the same latitude as Edinburgh. We went out to Kronborg (Elsinore) Castle, which always delights me, partly because it is maritime, but chiefly for its splendid baroque architecture (*circa* 1630), the sixteenth-century wood-carving in the chapel, the pictures and tapestries, and the great presence chamber, which I estimate to be a good 200 feet long (and upstairs at that!); the largest room known to me.

On the outer moat at Kronborg I saw a pen (female swan) on her nest. The cob (male) was at liberty and also on the outer moat; but beyond the gatehouse, on the inner moat, I noticed something rather curious. A light, low net had been stretched across the breadth of the moat (looking rather like a table-tennis net!). This was apparently intended to restrict another swan. Presumably this swan's wings were clipped, for as we came by he was swimming from side to side behind the net, obviously anxious to get past but unable to do so. When we returned that way, over an hour later, he was still at it, poor chap! I wonder why he had to be kept in with a net?

Plenty of swallows were skimming over the moat, and also sand martins. Some of the latter were building in cavities along the bricked, vertical sides of the moat.

Kronborg Castle –

8TH MAY

We went out to Dragør (pronounced 'Drow-oor'), a village not far from Copenhagen, originally a settlement for immigrant Dutch artisans. The date I would guess to be fairly early nineteenth century (*circa* 1830). The Dutch were encouraged to build the village in the style of their own country, and it is now preserved. The houses are wooden-shuttered, with brightly painted doors and window-frames and thatched or red-tiled roofs. Broad footpaths run between the cottages and gardens. Since the place is so quiet and the air so clean, the small gardens attract plenty of birds. I saw a blackcap (*Sylvia atricapilla*) in an apple tree, quite close to an open window. Nowadays, of course, blackcaps don't normally come close to houses: too much disturbance.

I also saw – and this really pleased me – a white wagtail (the continental sub-species of *Motacilla alba*, of which our pied wagtail is another sub-species). I had never seen one before. Initially, I recognized it as a wagtail, and then saw that it was not an ordinary pied wagtail. It had more white on the face, rather like a great tit, and although it had a black 'bib' and a black cap and tail, the belly and back were markedly light-coloured – a sort of greyish-fawn. It was behaving like a pied wagtail, however.

9TH MAY

To-day, at a village called Søllerod, we saw a horizontal wheel (three or three and a half feet in diameter) on top of the church tower. It is a fixture, its function being to provide a nesting-place for storks. Alas! hardly any storks now nest throughout all Denmark. Jarl said he did not believe there were twenty pairs. According to Dr Philip Burton, the number of storks in Europe is dwindling, despite protection in most countries. He attributes the decline chiefly to the use of insecticides in African wintering areas. The poison gets into the storks' food, e.g. locusts and grasshoppers.

10TH MAY

To-day, on a large, flat island about forty minutes' run in a motor-launch from Copenhagen, I saw avocets (*Recurvirostra avosetta*) for the first time in my life. Recognizing them in flight among the gulls, I literally danced with delight! They are fully as beautiful as photographs suggest: very graceful in flight, the legs trailing not unlike a heron's. From directly below they appear white, with black tips to the wings. The striking, black-and-white plumage comes into view only when you are to one side of them or, of course, if you see them on the ground. The upturned bill was what I first recognized – unique and unmistakable.

I also saw shelduck (*Tadorna tadorna*) on that island; half-goose and half-duck, as Dr Burton describes them. The red beak and green head are very conspicuous, as is also the broad, chestnut band running round the white breast and shoulders.

Walking near a village called Hillerød, I found a bedstraw I haven't come across before. (One of the Rubiaceae.) It was growing thickly in a typical Danish beech wood, though not yet in bloom. Its leaves were fuller and smoother than those of a common goose-grass or of the white or yellow bedstraw, but I don't think it was madder.

I also saw, in a garden, a low-growing plant with dark-red umbels of bloom, like a verbena, and leaves rather like a geranium. It had no scent, but the bloom certainly resembled that of a verbena.

11TH MAY

Returned to London. We found ourselves at once amid the full riot of May. Lilac, magnolia, laburnum, lime trees in bloom, and chestnut candles everywhere, both red and white. The weather is that of a perfect May. The thick, green leaves make one realize summer is fully come.

14TH MAY

Returning to the Isle of Man, found it a different place from that which I left on 6th May! Eight days of perfect weather have brought everything on dramatically.

In the evening, having taken Tetter back from Stewart (who has been kindly looking after him), I took him for a walk up the lane. For the first time this year I found myself walking up a leafy tunnel, foliage-scented and enclosed; no longer an open, windy lane. The ash trees are in leaf at last; and the air was full of the sweet-sour carrion scent of may. The sycamores are in bloom, too, and the mountain ashes are covered with flat, white umbels. All along the verges the dull-mauve blooms of the bush vetch (*Vicia sepium*) are thick. The wild garlic – ramsons (*Allium ursinum*) – which the Manx call 'Stinking Roger', is flowering all over the place.

Mars has now dropped back from Jupiter, and is at nine o'clock from it. Saturn still in Virgo.

wild garlic

15TH MAY

Walking with Tetter, first along the disused railway line and then along the cliff-path, saw a beautiful bush of reticulate willow (*Salix reticulata*) in bloom, spreading and flat; bright-yellow bird's-foot trefoil (*Lotus corniculatus*) everywhere; tormentil (*Potentilla erecta*); the yellow broom (*Cytisus scoparius*) now fully out, scented and drooping heavy with bloom; the first pink thrift (*Armeria maritima*) in bloom along the cliff; and, best of all, *Scilla verna*, the blue vernal squill. I've been watching for that for some time. ('Western coastal pastures,' says Keble Martin.) Blue tapestry stars among the short, cliff-top grass.

Scilla verna

17TH MAY

To London – still in perfect May weather – to address the Vegetarian Society symposium on the Canadian harp seal slaughter. I got carried away, and abused and vilified the Newfoundlanders and the Canadian High Commissioner from the platform. It was not ill-received – to say the least.

bird's-foot trefoil

18TH MAY

The little London back garden here – about sixteen or seventeen yards square – contains several beautiful plants hitherto unknown to me. There are two different kinds of *Hosta*; one with fairly dark-green, cream-edged leaves; the other a lighter, clearer green. They have lanceolate leaves about as long as my hand or a little shorter, and their charm lies in the burgeoning, rampant luxuriance of the plant. I'm told they have a pale-mauve flower in August. Then there is a white azalea (*Azalea palestrina*), scentless but prolific of bloom. Chiefly I am taken with something called *Astrantia*; the whole plant about two and a half feet high and eighteen inches across, leaves palmate, with delicate, green-white blooms, each about an inch wide or so, mostly in open clusters at or near the tops of the stems. This particular plant is very healthy, with fifteen or twenty stems in bloom. The general effect is charming, recalling Andrew Marvell:

> 'Annihilating all that's made
> To a green thought in a green shade.'

Elsewhere, in Chiswick, I saw a newly planted shrub, some of its ovate, roughish leaves green and some darker in colour. It looked a little like a newly planted hazel-nut tree. It had a label, '*Corylus max. purpurea*'. I must ask Clif about this, and about *Astrantia*. I wonder what *Astrantia* is? An anemone? It's a little like a Japanese anemone, but even more delicate and attractive.

Later: Notes after talking to Clif Dadd: *Corylus max. purpurea* is an ornamental hazel: the purple filbert. (Well, perhaps it wasn't very difficult to guess.) The 'blooms' of *Astrantia* are, in fact, inflorescence – that is, a cluster of minute blooms on a head. It is an umbellifer. *Astrantia major* is, in fact, a wild flower. (See Keble Martin, Plate 36.) The one in the Canonbury garden was probably *Astrantia carniolica*. Hostas, Clif thinks, are related to lilies, but he will check that too.

19TH MAY

Back in the Island, I was walking through St John's this afternoon, and stopped to admire lilac blooming in a garden. Then I saw a robin lying in the road. It was clearly dying; one eye injured; bleeding from the beak and gasping convulsively. I suppose I should have wrung its neck. It died in my hand about ten minutes later. Obviously someone must have hit it with a car or a motor-cycle. Did he know? Did he care? How sad to die in mid-May, in such glorious weather. *Miselle passer*! This quite spoilt the day.

20TH MAY

Dropping in to have a look at the cascade at Spooyt Vane this afternoon, I came upon one of my favourite wild flowers in full bloom: the yellow pimpernel (*Lysimachia nemorum*). I love it partly

yellow
pimpernel ~

Spooyt Vane

for the trim, cool, clean appearance of the prostrate plant, but chiefly for the smooth, clear yellow of the bloom itself. It likes damp, shady places. This particular plant was exactly where one would expect to find it; half-way down the steps leading to the pool at the foot of the cascade.

21ST MAY

This morning went to the Chasms and the high cliff above Bay Stacka, in the south of the Island. At the east end of Bay Stacka stands the Sugarloaf, an isolated, vertical pillar of rock, the height of which I would guess to be about a hundred feet. It is virtually sheer, although it tapers from the base. On its slate ledges and also on the ledges of the cliff near by were hundreds of razorbills (*Alca torda*). Most were sitting in the characteristic, upright posture which makes them look like little penguins. A good deal of mutual preening was going on.

Dr Burton says that razorbills, which make use of no nesting materials, lay in small caves in cliffs, or among boulders and scree, and that ledge laying is rare. The Manx slate cliffs opposite the Chasms are indented with ledges, one above another like bookshelves, and several of these are all of two to three feet deep, with low overhangs. One sees razorbills there every year at this time. I'd be surprised if some of them were not laying.

The razorbill is an auk; they lay a single egg 'in a cavity towards the top of a cliff or under boulders on the shore'. (Drive Publications, *Book of British Birds.*)

22ND MAY

Out on the cliffs again to-day, and found a great deal of sea-campion (*Silene maritima*) in full bloom. Each bloom is a rosette of about ten broad petals, overlapping and frilled. The anthers in the centre have black tips, which contrast prettily with the white, frilly, surrounding petals.

I also found on the cliff a sheep's-bit scabious (*Jasione montana*) with about fifteen blooms: first I've seen this year. I like the way the pink-tipped anthers stick up out of the blue, globular flower-heads.

A blackbird was still singing at ten past ten.

23RD MAY

To-night, as dusk was beginning to fall, I looked up from my desk and recognized the dark, back-swept shapes of swifts (*Apus apus*) on the wing. I opened the window so that I could hear them screaming. Dr Burton says they may fly 500 miles a day when hunting insects for their young. They catch flies by gaping as they dive and dart, and accumulate them, in their throat pouches, into balls glued with saliva. These are then regurgitated for the young.

The lake excavation is now complete and is filling with water naturally, at a rate of about six inches in twenty-four hours. It will be an impressive bit of water when it's complete – an irregular triangle, something like fifty yards long and perhaps twenty-five or thirty across at the broadest point. Pied wagtails and moorhens are already displaying an interest. Clif intends to start riparian planting next week.

24TH MAY

A good walk this afternoon, in fine, sunny weather with a cool breeze. Heard the chiff-chaff briefly; also yellowhammers and willow warblers. Saw the following wild flowers for the first time this year: in a ploughed field, dark-red fumitory (*Fumaria officinalis*), a weed of cultivation; or, as Fitter and Fitter have it, 'arable fields and waste places'. Also field forget-me-nots (*Myosotis arvensis*). In a meadow, several plants of milkwort (*Polygala vulgaris*) spreading their deep-blue upper petals like tiny wings. (Milkwort isn't always deep blue. It may be mauve, pink or even white.) In the now dried-

Sheepsbit Scabious

up marsh on Upper Lhergy Dhoo, a lot of pink lousewort (*Pedicularis sylvatica*) thriving despite the very dry weather.

To-night at sunset – about 21.40 hours – one could plainly see, with binoculars, that Venus was at half-phase in the west.

Burnet rose –

25TH MAY

The lake is filling slowly and steadily.

Elizabeth came on the East Lhergy Dhoo–Langtoft–Peel cliff-path walk this afternoon. There was quite a lot to be seen, in a quiet way, viz.: corn spurrey (*Spergula arvensis*), meadow vetchling (*Lathyrus pratensis*), wild raspberries in bloom (*Rubus idaeus*), the pale-yellow burnet rose (*Rosa pimpinellifolia*), very sweetly scented ('often on coastal dunes', Fitter), and the first white bedstraw, probably *Galium saxatile*, I should think, for it was very short, regularly *part of* the grass, on dry turf near the sea. The navelwort (*Umbilicus rupestris*), rife throughout the Island, is now showing its long, greenish spikes in bud.

Saw a rock pipit (*Anthus spinoletta*) – smoky in colour – along the cliff.

The ewes have all been shorn now, but their lambs, of course, have not. This makes them both look odd!

Plenty of wall butterflies out along the hedgerows. This will be the first brood. (There are two or even three broods in a season.)

27TH MAY

This evening I took a look out of the window at the half-filled lake, and saw a heron on the bank! As Elizabeth and I watched, it took a few steps down into the water. It didn't take long to realize there were no fish, took to its wings and flew away over the meadow. A foretaste of what we can expect when we start stocking, no doubt.

28TH MAY

Now we are arrived at the tall grass of summer. When I was a boy and had to go to boarding-school, I always felt it as a grievance that I left home in late April, before the grass was properly tall, and when I came back in late July they'd cut it all down. Robbed of ten years' tall summer grass and moon daisies!

I have several grasses in a vase on the desk, and very pretty they look: *Poa pratensis*, smooth meadow-grass; *Elymus repens*, couch-grass (or twitch); *Alopecurus pratensis*, fox-tail; *Lolium temulentum*, darnel; and *Eriophorum vaginatum*, the hare's-tail (what I call 'bog cotton') whose white, thistledown heads are to be seen all over the heathery moors just now.

29TH MAY (*Oakapple Day*)

Being uncertain about my identification, on 24th May, of the forget-me-not in the ploughed field as *Myosotis arvensis*, I went back to have another look. It *isn't Myosotis arvensis*. The little spikes of bloom curl right over at the top like a shepherd's crook. This has decided me that it can only be:

Myosotis discolor. Yellow Forget-me-not. (Keble Martin)
Myosotis discolor. Changing Forget-me-not. (Fitter and Fitter)
Myosotis versicolor. Yellow-and-Blue Forget-me-not. (Fitch and Smith)

These blooms are nowhere yellow, though, even though they're not far advanced: they're very pale blue. According to the books, they are supposed to start yellow and then change to blue. (Some of them *are* sort of white, though.) An interesting find.

30TH MAY

Heard a blackcap this morning. I fear he won't remain, however. Found silverweed (*Potentilla anserina*) in bloom in the cornfield: genus Rosaceae – in other words, it's one of the rose family. The silvery backs of the pinnate leaves are very attractive.

Elizabeth and I flew to London in the evening, to stay the weekend with Asa and Susan Briggs at Oxford. (Asa, an old friend, is now Provost of Worcester, my college.)

31ST MAY

Driving from London to Oxford, noticed thick clumps of ox-eye daisies (*Leucanthemum vulgare*) growing beside the motorway. Elizabeth pointed out that they grew on only one side of the road – the north side. I never thought of moon daisies as needing sunshine or strong light, but evidently they prefer a sunny aspect.

June

1ST JUNE

In the Provost's garden at Worcester stands what I suppose must be one of the finest hornbeam trees in the country. I reckon its height as all of seventy feet. My *Observer's Book of Trees and Shrubs* (W.J. Stokoe) says that when growing on low ground, in good soil, the hornbeam can be expected to reach seventy feet, with a girth of ten. All I can say is that I can't remember to have seen one to equal this.

It was pleasant, too, to see a really large Judas tree (redbud: *Cercis siliquastium*), covered with maroon-coloured bloom.

Met Iris Murdoch at lunch, and we talked for a good hour or more.

I looked at the Worcester College lake – which I've known for over forty years – with new eyes – the eyes of one who (almost) has a (much smaller) lake of his own! It is, of course, a superb lake: boomerang-shaped, each arm over 100 yards long, the breadth a good fifty yards at the broadest part; extensive, placid, graceful and majestic. Asa told me that not long ago a student from St John's did a 'fish count'. This showed over-population, and accordingly they stunned the fish (perch and roach mostly) painlessly and removed a lot of them to the adjacent canal: whence, he strongly suspected, they had made their way back into the lake.

Worcester College lake –

3RD JUNE

Drove down to Groombridge in Kent, to stay with Jim and Pam Rose at their beautiful cottage near Penn's House. (Penn the Quaker.) They took us to Glyndebourne in the evening. (Verdi's *Falstaff.*) The gardens were looking splendid.

At Jim's we had lunch out of doors, in an open-sided barn with an old, red-brick floor. Between the bricks was growing *Oxalis corniculata*, the yellow-flowered *Oxalis*, with its tawny, trefoil-leaved foliage. In southern England it's common in conservatories and between the stones and bricks of outdoor floors and paths. 'Naturalized,' says Keble Martin. 'Local,' says Hooker (1884). 'Possibly indigenous in S.W. England, not north of it.' He also says 'Waste shady places.' Well, I've *always* thought of it as growing particularly between bricks, by water-butts, etc.

Jim took me to see the garden of Penn's House. Masses of golden azaleas, growing virtually wild. The scent was wonderful. They cover the slopes of a knoll, on the summit of which is a stone arbour originally constructed by Dorothy Wellesley.

Oxalis corniculata –

4TH JUNE

This morning Pam Rose took Elizabeth and me to see the lake in the grounds of Penn's House. It is secluded, surrounded by trees, with a small, Grecian-style temple standing above it. It's more-or-less circular, and I suppose about forty yards across. Purple flags in bloom and meadow-sweet coming on. Saw a dragon-fly (green): almost certainly *Cordulia linaenea*.

I picked some rather striking, tall, white-blooming Cruciferae, which I later identified as *Cardamine amara*, the large bittercress. ('Flowers white, anthers purple. Moist meadows and riversides, local.' Keble Martin.)

Returned to the Isle of Man in the evening. Sultry and thundery all night. Heavy rain.

5TH JUNE

Saw a whitethroat (*Sylvia communis*) bathing in the shallow edge of the half-filled lake this morning. It made a thorough job of its bath, then flew up into the hawthorns and dried its wings by fluttering them rapidly for a long time.

Ronald Lockley 'phoned. He's arrived in this country and is on his way to the Orkneys.

6TH JUNE

Suddenly the Island is full of painted lady butterflies! Walking up Peel Hill this afternoon, I saw one on the turf, and delightedly pointed it out to my companions. But then we saw another – and twenty minutes later, along the cliffs, another. They are easily startled, and fly quickly and twistingly, with very rapid movement of their pink wings, to a fresh resting-place, usually on the ground. To-day and also on 7th June, walking first on the west and then on the east coasts of the Island, I saw many – some battered-looking, others fresh and bright. Mr Stokoe says: 'It is a notorious [*sic*] migrant' (sounds as if it were absconding!) 'and its proper home is probably Northern Africa ... It quits the land of its birth in swarms.'

Guillemots –

Shags

cliff edge –

Later: I quote from Dr Jiri Zahradnik: 'Flies a zig-zag course on dry fields. A migrant. Arrives in . . . northern Europe from the south, April to May. Progeny usually return south in autumn. Caterpillar favours nettle, thistle, coltsfoot.' So they *do* breed here, as well as in North Africa. Who'd have expected such fragile creatures to fly hundreds of miles north – and then south again?

7TH JUNE

Between Cashtal yn Ard and Port Cornaa, in a shady, damp spot, I came upon a large patch of *Montia sibirica*, the pink purslane; a pretty wild flower, rather like a succulent, pink stitchwort. (I recall finding it in a brook on Hampstead Heath some years ago.) It spreads along little brooks, open ditches and the like. It's not indigenous – naturalized from North America, say Fitter and Fitter. The blooms close up at night and also in wet weather. I brought some home and have it in water on my desk. Being almost aquatic by nature, it should last a long time. (*Later*: It did.)

pink purslane

8TH JUNE

Honeysuckle (*Lonicera periclymenum*) blooming in the hedge along the lane. Also *Sedum anglicum*, the English stonecrop.

Walking from Peel to Glenmaye, saw a great number of guillemots (*Uria aalge*) perching on the almost vertical side of a big rock at the foot of the cliff. Several small flotillas of guillemots were cruising some distance from the shore. They fly with very rapid wing-beats: indeed, they can be recognized by this at a distance.

Also saw a common seal close inshore.

Kittiwakes

Guillemots

9TH JUNE

Down near Blue Point – a sandy, shingly beach on the north-west coast, sloping gently to rough grassland behind – I watched ringed plovers (*Charadrius hiaticula*) and came upon several nests. They have a Walt Disney-ish appearance; pretty little faces, black-and-white, with a white collar and black bib below. It's difficult to spot them among the stones of a shingly beach, for they rely on camouflage, and will often sit tight until you're no more than twenty yards away. There are usually two or three together, and they fly off low and swiftly, twirling and showing dark-and-light in flight over the sea. At this time of year one often comes upon their 'nests'. Four eggs as a rule, laid in some slight recess among the stones, pointed ends inward. They're buff, mottled dark, and tone in with the shingle. When you find one, the birds kick up an awful shine, flying round and round. I take the hint and move on.

78

10TH JUNE

An amusing incident down on the Chasms this afternoon. I was sitting on the edge of the cliff, watching the fulmars gliding up and back to the sheer ledges of another cliff about forty yards away. Other fulmars, and also herring gulls, were ensconced along the sheltered, overhung ledges. A kestrel (*Falco tinunculus*) appeared and alighted on an empty ledge about half-way down the cliff-face. Thereupon both fulmars and gulls gave it no peace, but 'buzzed' it continually, screaming and making as though to attack. The kestrel stuck it for about fifteen minutes, but finally flew sulkily away.

11TH JUNE

A wet day, with low cloud and light but thundery rain. As I was walking in the lanes this evening with Tetter, the thrushes were shouting and snails were out everywhere. I picked quite a few off the surface of the road and put them in the long grass.

All I have on snails is the *Encyclopaedia Britannica*. I gather that these snails were *Helix nemoralis* or perhaps *Helix hortensis*. 'The animals, being hermaphrodite, copulate reciprocally.' Another bit of scientific Humpty-Dumptyism. Don't we all copulate reciprocally? (At least, that's the ideal, quite often realized.)

I guess it means that the male bit of snail A fertilizes the female bit of snail B, what time the male bit of snail B . . .

12TH JUNE

The wet spell continues, with low, dark, oppressive cloud and still weather. Rather trying for walking. What consolations? Well, the chaps laying a new sewer-pipe in my little wood happened to find a whitethroat's nest in the undergrowth. They reported it, so that we could treat it with appropriate respect. Long grass plus a bit of horsehair. Only two eggs as yet, sort of olive, blotched dark blue. I shall leave it strictly alone, of course.

13TH JUNE

More consolations. The *Cotoneaster horizontalis* is covered with little globular, pink blooms, now turning to fruit. Although not at all fragrant to human nostrils, the shrub is covered – nay, crawling – with bumble-bees and bees. They are all over it from dawn to dusk. 'Well,' said Clif Dadd when I asked him, 'we don't know, do we, what fragrancy wavelength they're on?'

14TH JUNE

Everywhere throughout the Island one now sees, like flowering may (only less attractive), great, white patches of the shrub *Olearia macrodonta*. It is popular here as a wind-break for gardens, being evergreen (with a slightly thorny, holly-like leaf). At this time of year it blooms thickly. Its common name is 'Australian holly', and this reminds me of Voltaire: 'Ni saint, ni romain, ni empire.' It is, in fact, neither Australian nor a holly. It is a Composita and comes from New Zealand.

15TH JUNE

Down near the Tynwald Mills I came upon a neat device for topping a wall with flowering plants. An ordinary, dry-stone garden wall is topped with flat slates. Along either edge are bedded angle-irons. The shallow trough so formed is filled with earth – about an inch to an inch and a half in depth. This will take anything, of course – pansies, aubretia, arabis, etc. What it has at the moment is pendent trails of deep-pink *Saponaria ocymoides*, 'Tumbling Ted'; very pretty.

16TH JUNE

It continues to rain on and off – showery weather, disappointing for midsummer.

The lake is now almost full, and should be entirely so within the fortnight. A pied wagtail has taken up a habitat about the shore and on the island in the middle. The willow warbler sings all day in the willow grove at the south end.

17TH JUNE

There seem to be plenty of red admirals about the Island. I love the touches of blue along the outer edge of the fore-wings and at the bottoms of the hind-wings: also the wavy margins of the wings, like the edge of a postage stamp.

18TH JUNE

Plenty of wild orchids in bloom now, especially along shady banks and wet spots in meadows. I haven't stumbled on anything uncommon, however. Just the early purple (*Orchis mascula*), the common spotted (*Dactylorhiza fuchsii*) and the pyramidal (*Anacamptis pyramidalis*).

orchis mascula

19TH JUNE

Along the river Neb, at Ballig, the common valerian (*Valeriana officinalis*) is blooming thickly; tall, slender, pale pink, beautifully scented, moving in the wind. Also called 'all-heal', 'cut-finger' and 'cat's love'. (Apparently cats like the scent of the dry root. I must try it on ours. What used the roots to be dried for, I wonder?) 'Valerian tea,' says Geoffrey Grigson, 'is taken to calm the head, to prevent hysteria, etc.' Of the smell of the dried root, he says, 'Not very pleasant: like new leather, yet foetid.'

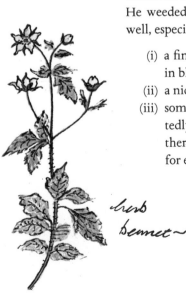

Common Valerian

20TH JUNE

This afternoon I was somewhat surprised to see a blackcap sitting exposed on a telegraph wire. He was singing – not a full song: a bit of a sub-song; but he *was* singing. After a little he flew down into the bushes, but soon returned to the telegraph wire. Unusual for a blackcap?

22ND JUNE

Our chap who comes to weed the big border outside the front of the house seems, like me, to have a selective taste for wild flowers. He weeded away like mad to-day and cleared the whole border well, especially the hemlock and ragwort. However, he left:

(i) a fine plant of herb bennet or wood avens (*Geum urbanum*) in bloom.
(ii) a nice, big cushion of white clover.
(iii) some plants of figwort (*Scrophularia nodosa*), which admittedly look very much as though they were meant to be there. (Not being in bloom, the plants might be mistaken for e.g. bergamot.)

herb bennet

23RD JUNE

Everywhere along the banks and edges of the woods are clumps of foxgloves, with bumble-bees disappearing into the blooms and reappearing backwards. I love a *white* foxglove, and have seen quite a few.

My American friend Lowell Wine arrived from Virginia, and will be staying a fortnight, to walk. He's never before been out of America! We were great walking companions ('trail buddies'!) in the Blue Ridge Mountains in 1976, and this is the return fixture.

The lake needs only about another foot of water to be full.

white foxglove

24TH JUNE

Lowell and I went out this afternoon, in beautiful weather, starting our walk across the moor west of Slieau Maggle, Colden and Lhargee Ruy; then down the Blaber valley and Glen Helen, and so home by Ballavaish. About seven miles. The larks were rising and falling, and the heather is just coming out. Lowell was delighted with both. The first heather he saw – had ever seen – was, actually, the cross-leaved heath (*Erica tetralix*) which comes out a little before the bell heather (*Erica cinerea*). There was a great deal more to delight a newcomer from Virginia, of course, but the only other things I'll note here are first, a fine show of eyebright (*Euphrasia officinalis*) in the meadow above Glen Helen, and a pair of grey wagtails in the glen itself.

25TH JUNE

Lowell very proud of his newly acquired terms. 'Heather', 'Glen', 'Moor', 'Tholtan', etc. (A 'tholtan' in Manx is a lonely rural dwelling – often abandoned, nowadays – usually on moor or upland meadow.)

Janice walked with us to-day (so did Tetter, of course) from St John's to Peel, down the valley of the lower Neb. The yellow irises (*Iris pseudacorus*) were blooming thickly in the water-meadows. I also observed my favourite vetch, the tufted vetch (*Vicia cracca*) (the fairies' hearth-brush): beautifully vivid purple bloom. Meadow-sweet not out as yet.

The broom is over and the bushes are thick with dry, black pods. As you pass, you hear them cracking in the sun.

cross-leaved heath

83

26TH JUNE

To-day Lowell and I did the Peel–Glenmaye–Slieau Whallian–St John's walk. Lowell enjoyed watching the guillemots below the cliffs. I saw a black guillemot (*Cepphus grylle*) on the sea near Peel Castle. The summer plumage is very handsome, I always think, with the conspicuous white wing-patches.

27TH JUNE

To-day I took Lowell to see the neolithic stone burial site at Cashtal yn Ard, after which we walked down Dhoon Glen to the cove and back up the cliff. The sanicles (*Sanicula europaea*) were blooming thickly in shady parts of the glen.

Burial site at
Cashtal-yn-Ard

To finish the day's outing, I took Lowell through Gob-ny-Deigan, the antral tunnel on the beach of the west coast, some three and a half miles north of Peel. This is a natural tunnel, perhaps seventy yards long, through the living rock of a promontory. At low tide one can walk through it from one beach to the next. Having reached the further beach, we saw a seal in the water, close inshore.

I was hoping the brookweed (*Samolus valerandi*) might be in bloom on the cliff-path, but as yet it isn't.

Gob - ny - Deigan -

28TH JUNE

Saw a parent wren fly out of the scrub willow this morning, followed by about five fledgling wrens. They were so *very* small! A pretty sight.

29TH JUNE

This afternoon Lowell and I climbed the east face of North Barrule, from Ballagilley to the summit; a matter of some 1,300 feet, I suppose, and pretty steep. Lowell, at sixty-two, is better on ascents than I at sixty. It's all his practice in the mountains of Colorado! On the ridge we encountered a cold north wind, with mist driven before it, but forged on nevertheless, climbed Clagh Ouyr and so down to Black Hut, where Elizabeth picked us up. Saw little on the tops but hares, which Tetter chased in vain.

Off to the Lakes to-morrow. I'm glad the weather has remained good for Lowell's stay. He's obviously enjoying the visit. It's gratifying to make some return for the Blue Ridge Mountains.

30TH JUNE

June goes out in pouring rain. We spent the day travelling across by boat to the Lake District. Arrived at our destination, Broughton-in-Furness, for dinner.

July

~ *looking down on Wastwater* ~

1ST JULY

The mist was well down on the tops this morning, which gave me the problem of how best to introduce Lowell to Lake District walking. We wouldn't be able to get up high with any worthwhile visibility. In the event, my solution worked well. We took the car up the Duddon valley, turned westward over Ulpha Fell to Eskdale Green and left the car at Keyhow. Thence we walked up Mitredale, on to Tongue Moor and climbed Illgill Head. From here Lowell got a fine view of the Screes and of Wastwater, 1,700 feet below, though he couldn't, unfortunately, see the summits of Gable or Scafell for mist. We walked back above Wastwater, by Whin Rigg and Irton Fell.

2ND JULY

To borrow a phrase from Mr Jorrocks, we've had a *buster*! The day promised well, and about 10.15 a.m. we set off to climb Walna Scar (2,035 feet) from the Seathwaite side. We were up in forty-five minutes and then went along the ridge to Dow Crag. Lowell photographed away like a true American.

We went round to Coniston Old Man (2,633 feet), back over Brim Fell and up Great How Crags to Swirral and on to Great Carrs. We lunched below Carrs, then climbed the Grey Friar and so down by way of Seathwaite Tarn.

Seathwaite
Tarn

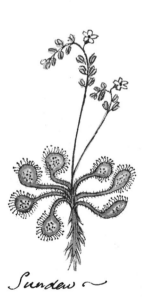

Sundew

On the high fells I found plenty of starry saxifrage (*Saxifraga stellaris*) blooming in the becksides and peat-hags: starry white, with red anthers, the bloom rising on a very thin stalk above a rosette of leaves. You don't find many flowers in bloom at 2,500 feet, but you do find that.

We saw swifts hunting above the range, at a height of something like 2,700 feet.

3RD JULY

My old friend, Roy Greenwood, now vicar of Penny Bridge, a tremendous mountaineer, came out with us to-day. The weather was excellent, but Roy had to go back soon after 3 p.m., so we settled for climbing Harter Fell (2,140 feet), an old favourite.

I always enjoy the approach to Harter from Duddon. From the road we went down through the fern to Fickle Steps, crossed Duddon into the forest and so up to Grassguards. The air was scented with bog myrtle, and the yellow bog asphodel (*Narthecium ossifragum*) was in bloom everywhere. From the top of Harter we had a splendid view of Eskdale, the Scafell range and the Roman fort on Hard Knott.

Lots of sundews (*Drosera rotundifolia*) all over the fells, but oddly I saw none in bloom. (The blooming period is June–August.)

In the Duddon valley, near Birks Bridge, we watched two or three whinchats flitting about (*Saxicola rubetra*).

After Roy left us, Lowell and I spent the later afternoon climbing Caw, starting from the Newfield Inn. Much better fun than I expected. It's best ascended from the south side, as the southern rock slopes near the summit are quite dramatic.

4TH JULY

My goodness, what a day! We set out to climb Crinkle Crags, and reached Cockley Beck by car about 10.15 a.m. The Red How, of course, is a hard pull up, through fern and rock, some 2,000 feet above Cockley Beck. We took about an hour over it, and when we got up found the tops misty. The mist thickened, and by the time we'd walked the length of the Crinkles and reached Three Tarns, visibility was down to about sixty yards.

I never like mist on the tops. Apart from the threat that it may close down altogether at any moment, the mere sight of the mist,

88

swirling round the precipices of black rock, is sinister and demoralizing. You feel it's malevolent and means you no good. (My friend Dennis Williamson, as tough a Lakeland sheep-farmer as one could well hope to meet, has told me that he also feels this malevolence in mist.) I would have preferred to pack it in, and go down from Three Tarns into Green Hole below, but Lowell was main set on climbing Bow Fell. It seemed a pity to disappoint an honest Virginian, so I let myself be persuaded.

The mist grew thicker as we went up, and near the summit there came on a driving rain which soon had us wet through, despite our quilted jackets. We held on, by compass and cairn, over Esk Pike. The Esk Hause seemed a damned long time coming, I'll tell thee! At last we came upon a beck flowing down to the left.

'Down this beck we will now go,' said I firmly, 'and nee messin' aboot.'

'D'you figure maybe we should look arahnd for a trail leading dahn?' inquired Lowell (whose morale remained excellent).

'No!' said I. 'We will get below this mist with all possible celerity!'

We went down the course of the beck – in and out of it, but by then it didn't matter: we couldn't be wetter. After about forty minutes we got below the mist, saw Cam Spout in the distance, and began the plod back to Cockley Beck over Yeastyrigg Crags – a good five miles, I reckon. Boots wet, clothes wet; but at least we weren't cold.

I think this is about the most inclement day on the tops I can recall – ever. Lowell said he sure wouldn't have missed the experience! He could have had mine as well.

Lowell is an excellent walking companion – or 'trail buddy', to use his own phrase. Staunch, you might say. I hope to walk with him in Colorado next year.

5TH JULY

More bad weather to-day, so we went to see the Waters of Lodore (which I always reckon ought to be spelt 'Low Door', pace Robert Southey) at the southern end of Derwentwater.

The place was stiff with cars. As we were coming down the road (B5289) east of Derwentwater itself, I was delighted to see a red squirrel (*Sciurus vulgaris leucourus*) run across the road in the direction of the lake. It leapt up on the low stone wall, paused a

moment, then ran along it and jumped down on the other side, out of sight.

'Let's go and see whether we can get another sight of it,' said I to Lowell.

We stopped the car, crossed the road, walked back a little way and looked for S. Nutkin. (Derwentwater is, I rather think, the lake depicted by Beatrix Potter in that great work.) No luck. When we got back, we found we'd created a major traffic problem.

'Can't stop 'ere!'

'What th'ell reckon you're doin'?' etc., etc.

Words fail me.

Rosebay willow-herb (*Epilobium angustifolium*) is now in bloom all over the place, so summer's getting on.

Saw several tree-creepers (*Certhia familiaris*) at Low Door.

6TH JULY

Lowell and I returned to Knocksharry to find Ronald Lockley already arrived and, like Tommy Brock, sitting at Mr Tod's kitchen table, pouring out tea from Mr Tod's tea-pot into Mr Tod's tea-cup. He told us he'd already seen a sparrow-hawk in the wood, and several ravens over the house.

7TH JULY

Lowell left for Virginia via Dublin this morning.

In the afternoon Ronald and I went for a shortish walk by lanes and the sea, and observed: three or four whitethroats along the Switchback lane; a pair of stonechats near the sea, the cock very smart; and a sand martin (*Riparia riparia*) flying over the beach.

Saw the following wild flowers in bloom for the first time this year: harebells (*Campanula rotundifolia*), a great mullein (*Verbascum thapsus*), some restharrow (*Ononis repens*) and a beautiful little plant of pink centaury (*Centaurium erythraea*).

Along the cliff-top, Ronald pointed out a buckshorn plantain (*Plantago coronopus*) and a sea plantain (*Plantago maritima*) and showed me the difference.

— harebells

— pink centaury

Ronald has observed a movement southward, down the Island, of chaffinches. He's seen a great many among the tops of the conifers up in the wood. Clif Dadd, consulted, says he has also observed them, and points out that while *en route* they are eating quantities of young caterpillars, aphids and parasites on the tender extremities of the trees.

This afternoon Ronald and I walked along the sandy, north-west beach towards Blue Point. There was any amount to be seen. Plenty of Arctic terns (*Sterna paradisaea*) and also the rarer Little terns (*Sterna albifrons*), distinguishable by smaller size (oddly enough) and by the white patch on the forehead, which shows up plainly in flight. There was also a small group of four or five dunlins (*Calidris alpina*) running about and feeding in the sandy pools. These were clearly identifiable by the black patch covering the lower breast (summer plumage), but Ronald was puzzled by two similar wading birds with shorter beaks and *white* underparts, which moved away from the main group as we approached. He was sure they were of another species, but couldn't decide what. I thought perhaps they might be sanderlings (*Calidris alba*) but Ronald said it wasn't likely that sanderlings would be here at this time of year. The books don't help. Curlew sandpiper (*Calidris ferruginea*) and Baird's sandpiper (*Calidris bairdii*) both seem improbable. The two waders remain mysterious.

~ Common & little Terns at Blue Point ~

9TH JULY

The nuthatch still frequents the ash tree. Ronald pointed out to me that the Manx Museum's pamphlet *Birds of the Isle of Man*, published in 1975, doesn't list the nuthatch.

Pat Keysell arrived to-night, to stay for a few days. She's always keen to walk and watch birds.

10TH JULY

Out on the cliffs south of Peel this afternoon, we saw several puffins (*Fratercula arcula*), both flying and on the water: the first I've seen this summer. As we were watching a mass of guillemots covering the long slope of a big, tilted rock below, Ronald pointed out two kittiwakes (*Rissa tridactyla*) sitting on their nests: slighter in build than the gulls, with more graceful heads. The black-tipped primaries (wing tips) were noticeable, even though the birds were sitting. A great black-backed gull (*Larus marinus*) was hanging about in a nasty, sinister manner: no doubt, thought Ronald, on the chance of snatching an egg or a chick.

Also seen for the first time this year – a favourite of mine – the dull-pink bog pimpernel (*Anagallis tenella*) flowering all over a wet bank. I love the way it forms quite extensive, flat patches of bloom over its miniature, frond-like trails of leaves.

In bud: St John's wort, but heaven knows which one. If I had to guess, I'd say probably the slender (*Hypericum pulchrum*), because of the red tingeing. And a big clump of hemp agrimony (*Eupatorium cannabinum*). Both flowers of later summer, oh dear! The evenings are closing in perceptibly earlier, too. Summer seems already well past the solstice.

11TH JULY

Ronald left this morning. He's going to Bardsey Island for a week before joining John Guest, Stewart Kneale and myself at Bangor for the Manchester University extra-mural bird-watching course.

Pat Keysell and I walked from Kirk Michael to Orrisdale and back by the beach. We saw two ravens on the sandy cliff-face. On the sand above the shore we found the sea bindweed (*Calystegia soldanella*) in bloom: large, pink, white-striped flowers almost as showy as those of the common, white hedge bindweed – that curse of gardeners. Also plenty of sea spurge (*Euphorbia paralias*).

I saw a gannet (*Sula bassana*) well out to sea: the first I've seen this year. It pleased me to recognize the characteristic flight-behaviour, and the pointed, zigzag-shaped, black-tipped wings.

12TH JULY

Pat left this morning – back to London and the handicapped children for whom she's doing so much.

In the afternoon Stewart and I walked up the Corony valley, south of the North Barrule ridge, and then climbed it. At the top a cold rain came down, so two little penguins went quickly home again. However, before that happened we came upon the moorland or round-leaved crowfoot (*Ranunculus omiophyllus*) blooming in a peaty ditch. 'Floating leaves only,' says Keble Martin, 'divided half-way into three rounded, crenate segments.' ('Crenate' = with marginal teeth.) The leaves are quite as attractive as the white flower, I reckon. Fitter and Fitter, I observe, give rather short shrift to the water *Ranunculi* – hardly any pictures at all. Keble Martin does better here.

Riddle by Ronald Lockley: 'What did the Dandy Lie On?' Answer: 'Couch-grass.'

13TH JULY

A hot, still day. Flies in the bracken: a curse when walking. Yarrow, wood sage, mallow and such common flowers. Bales of hay piled in the new-cut, green fields. Yellowhammers and whitethroats in the gorse. High summer now.

In the lake: a resident moorhen. The lesser spearwort (*Ranunculus flammula* – possibly sub-species *scoticus*) in bloom along the margins

bog pimpernel ~

in places. And the first observed aquatic life! A lot of small, water-boatmen-like beetles sculling around in the shallows. Clif has ordered a hundred golden orfe! (A 'very active' fish, he says.)

14TH JULY

In bloom in the garden of 'Thie-ny-Struan', down Brack-a-Broom lane, by the Neb ford: the first dahlias (mostly Coltness singles, but also some bigger doubles), sweet peas and a most striking, pure-white clematis with masses of bloom.

There was cloudy pollution all down the course of the Neb this afternoon. I couldn't smell it, but it was ugly to see. The trout, however, seemed unaffected and were rising as usual.

15TH JULY

The ideal cottage garden (1st January *et seq.*) in Brack-a-Broom lane is a delight. Broad beans as tall as I, onions thriving, various brassicas all in rows, the shallots lifted and drying on the path, potatoes positively rampant. Monkshood in bloom, and an old grey pussy-cat sunning himself in one corner. Hooded bindweed all over the hedges, but what of it?

16TH JULY

I was driving the car up the Switchback lane this evening, when a lizard slithered rapidly across the road and disappeared into the fern. This, I feel sure, must have been *Lacerta vivipara*, the common lizard. It was about five or six inches long, and very thin in appearance.

Later, along the verge of the cornfield on the cliff-top below the house, I saw a good deal of corn marigold (*Chrysanthemum segetum*), splendidly showy, brilliant yellow.

18TH JULY

More rain all day, but on going out I came upon the first flowering toadflax (*Linaria vulgaris*). The long, curved, tapering spurs are strikingly graceful, and I like the primrose and saffron antirrhinum blooms.

19TH JULY

To-day Stewart and I crossed to Liverpool, to go to the Manchester University extra-mural summer school at Bangor. We are on the 'Sea-Birds in North Wales' course until 25th July.

As we approached Betws-y-Coed there was a spectacular view across the Conway valley – mountains and forested gorges – and great clouds of mist were rising here and there out of the pine forests. I was impressed, in the storm and mist, by the huge, fallen rocks lying beside the road in the Llanberis Pass. Snowdon is a harsher, steeper range than either the Scafell or Coniston ranges. I doubt I could tackle it now.

Here at Bangor, tutsan (*Hypericum androsaemum*) is in bloom everywhere; and in a flower-bed I have seen the first outdoor calceolarias of the year.

ragged
robin –

Great crested Grebe
+ young –

The course began this morning and we are all very much pleased
with the first day, for which the weather was cool and fine, if a
shade windy.

'In the field' we saw:

Wild flowers in bloom (I omit ones already seen this year and
noted in this diary): ragged robin (*Lychnis flos-cuculi*). (Odd that I
shouldn't have seen one earlier this year.) Wood cranesbill
(*Geranium sylvaticum*); hedge bedstraw (*Galium mollugo*); wild pansy
(*Viola tricolor*); two kinds of centaury, common and lesser (*Centaurea
erythraea* and *Centaurea pulchellum*); evening primrose (*Oenothera
erythrosepala*); viper's bugloss (*Echium vulgare*); weld (a mignonette
– *Reseda luteola*); yellow horned poppy (*Glaucium flavum*); reflexed
stonecrop (yellow, on walls, etc., *Sedum reflexum*); yellow sea lupin
(this doesn't seem to be in either Fitter or Keble Martin. I wonder
why not?); marsh lousewort (*Pedicularis palustris*). And finally, the
northern marsh orchid (*Dactylorchis purpurella*), most spectacular,
and very profuse. Tall, and a vivid purple in colour.

Moths, etc.: a red-and-black burnet moth (on a burnet rose);
Cinnabar caterpillars on the ragwort.

Birds: (a) *On inland waters* – reed bunting (*Emberiza schoeniclus* –
in the reeds, of course); great crested grebe and young (*Podiceps
cristatus*); little grebe (*Tachybaptus ruficollis*); a pair of shelduck and
young (*Tadorna tadorna*); Canada geese (*Branta canadensis*); and a
ruddy duck (*Oxyura jamaicensis*). This duck, which is small, has a
white chin and throat, russet plumage for the rest, and a very
noticeable, pale-blue beak. We were told that it was originally
imported from Jamaica to Slimbridge (presumably by Sir Peter
Scott), bred, and released. It is now breeding quite happily in the
wild in England.

(b) *On the sea*: Manx shearwaters (*Puffinus puffinus*); Sandwich
tern (*Sterna sandvicensis*); Roseate tern. (I omit such previously
noted and familiar things as cormorants, shags, oyster-catchers,
etc.)

We watched, for some time, along the shores of the Ynys
Llanddwyn peninsula, a number of roseate terns (*Sterna dougallii*)
fishing for sand eels in the shallow bay. This, I think, was the best
sight of the day for me, since I had never seen roseate terns before.
(I don't find it easy to distinguish the roseate from the Arctic tern.
However, here goes: the roseate tern has a longer tail, a longer,

black beak, red at the base; shorter wings, longer legs and whiter plumage.)

Coming home in the 'bus, we passed a red squirrel dead in the road, and a magpie picking it over. Killed by a car, I suppose.

21ST JULY

The course continues enjoyable. Cool, fine weather, pleasant companions, excellent instructor (Richard Arnold), plenty of birds (and, incidentally, good food).

This morning we had some interesting instruction on why sea-birds nest in colonies, the differing natures of such colonies and their relationship to the birds' feeding-habits and feeding-grounds. Too long to reproduce here, but I feel more knowledgeable for it.

Sea aster –

Wild flowers seen to-day include: the sea aster (*Aster tripolium*), a pretty mauve Composita, growing along the shore of an estuary; sea lavender (*Limonium vulgare*); purple loosestrife (*Lythrum salicaria*). (You'd wonder I haven't seen any earlier.) Agrimony (*Agrimonia eupatoria*) (not to be confused with the pink, hemp agrimony, to which it is not related, of course); water mint (*Mentha aquatica*); common skullcap (*Scutellaria galericulata*), whose bright-blue flowers make it rather a favourite of mine; red bartsia (*Odontites verna*); and fleabane (*Pulicaria dysenterica*), but only in bud.

We also saw three distinctly unusual wild flowers, viz.:

(a) *Ostera nana*, the dwarf eel-grass. This, so Richard Arnold told us, is the only flowering plant that grows in the sea. (It is actually one of those between-the-tides things, covered twice a day. It was growing on the mud-flats of an estuary called the Inland Sea, uncovered at low tide.)

(b) The spatulate fleawort (*Senecio spathulifolius*).

(c) The spotted rock-rose (*Tuberaria guttata*, sub-species *breweri*).

Now to the birds. We went first to the Inland Sea, at a place called Four Mile Bridge. Here, splashing through fairly deep, glutinous low-tide mud, we watched a lot of redshanks (*Tringa totanus*) feeding, as well as some bar-tailed godwits (*Limosa lapponica*) and dunlins. We made our very muddy way out to a rock where a colony of Arctic terns (*Sterna paradisaea*) were nesting. They 'buzzed' us, screaming, as is their wont. The chicks, however, seemed quite unafraid. I picked one up and it sat calmly in my

redshanks –

hand, needing no restraint. When I put it down it didn't run away, although it was mobile enough to do so. The big rock was covered all over with eggs, but several were smashed and some cold; and we also saw a dead tern. Evidence of raids by predators – rats or foxes – Arnold said. He also told us that there are only about 1,000 pairs of terns of all species breeding in North Wales; and these are the only terns breeding between the Scilly Isles and North Lancashire (not counting the Isle of Man).

There were several herons on the estuary. At one moment I had three in the sights of my binoculars.

Passing some pine-woods near by, we saw several redpolls (*Acanthis flammea*). I had never seen this bird before and was struck by its beauty. One was sitting on top of a pine tree, facing me head-on. I must have been about 150 yards away. It appeared, in my binoculars, almost like a rosy lovebird – a dusky rose-colour across the breast, flushed deeper in the centre. They fly flirtingly, up and down, like pipits, and have a twittering cry.

We went on to South Stack, Holyhead Island. Here I saw (when Arnold had told me what they were) two hybrid crows, half hooded crow and half carrion crow. Apparently there is what is called a Hybrid Zone, no more than forty or fifty miles across, extending from South Scotland across to Jutland and thence southward across Europe, within which these two kinds of crow interbreed. These two hybrids, therefore, must have come a good bit south of their birthplace. The zone seems an interesting ornithological phenomenon.

I also saw a pretty, small blue butterfly which the warden told me was a Silver Studded Blue; and watched, through a telescope, a razorbill·preening its chick on a nesting ledge. They seemed so much absorbed in each other that I couldn't help feeling rather moved.

Met with a drop-out racing pigeon walking about on top of the cliff. It wouldn't let any of us pick it up, so we had to leave it.

22ND JULY

I suppose if you're *looking* for signs of autumn you see them. To-day I observed: mountain ash berries, very orange on the bough; phlox in bloom in a front garden – both white and carmine. I smelt it, too – that highly evocative smell of late summer. And a sunflower, a good seven feet high.

Another splendid day, despite rather strong wind. As we set out (after a most interesting lecture on the British auks, and the correspondence between burrowing habits and lengthier periods of incubation and fledging, as opposed to non-burrowing auks such as razorbills), we stopped to watch greylag geese (*Anser anser*) feeding in a meadow. These geese, apparently, are a problem in Anglesey, for there are a lot, and three of them eat as much as one sheep!

On an inland lake called Llywenan, we watched (despite the wind) teal (*Anas crecca*), pochard (*Aythya ferina*), shovellers (*Anas clypeata*) and (the best in my judgement) a pair of whooper swans (*Cygnus cygnus*), majestic, with great yellow bills and buff-coloured heads.

whooper Swans —

We stopped to see a fourteenth-century water mill at Melin Howell, and here we found (in the mill-race) *Stachys palustris*, the marsh woundwort. It's not uncommon, according to the book, yet I can't remember to have seen it before; a tall, mauve-flowered, riparian labiate.

On Camlyn lagoon we saw a red-breasted merganser duck (*Mergus serrator*) and eight chicks (the chicks coping imperturbably with windy, choppy water); and then, delightfully, were able to watch Sandwich terns (*Sterna sandvicensis*) through the telescope. I could see plainly the black, yellow-tipped beak which distinguishes them (principally) from Arctic and Common terns. It was amusing to watch their young learning to fly – five yards at a time, struggling, followed by an enforced pause. ('Why *can't* I do it – *he* can?' How well I know that feeling!)

There was also a golden plover (*Pluvialis apricaria*) on the shores of the terns' island. A big bird – as big as a pigeon. It really *is* speckled golden, has a black patch on the stomach (like a dunlin) and a dark patch behind the eye. It would be in passage, Richard Arnold said – an early migrant, perhaps from the Scotch moors.

Then – and this, for me, was the best sight of the day – we watched an intermittent train of Manx shearwaters in flight westward, about 200 yards out to sea, making their way against the wind, beating out of Liverpool bay towards Bardsey. Their flight is remarkable; wheeling, soaring, dipping and irregular, the birds appearing alternately dark and light as they turn in the air.

Ronald Lockley tells me that this marvellously beautiful flight is due to the birds' use of air currents. The wind affords them the power to rise, yet also slows them down. They rise on an air

manx Shearwaters —

current, but then descend faster. They never actually strike the waves, because the few inches of air between the wing and the waves exert pressure, creating an air cushion which repels the descending bird. This steady though irregular procession of shearwaters out at sea, all flying in the same direction, had about it an almost ritual character, at once arbitrary and inevitable.

I also watched turnstones (*Arenaria interpres*) on the tidal rocks. They are a little smaller than oyster-catchers, white-bellied, vividly brown-speckled above, with orange legs. In flight they display a white wing-bar. They don't breed in Britain, but in the far north.

Coming back in the evening, saw a whimbrel (*Numenius phaeopus*) in a meadow: shorter-billed than a curlew. They occur on the Isle of Man, I suppose. I must look out for them.

Wild flowers: sea kale (*Crambe maritima*); great lettuce (*Lactuca virosa*). This is a big, maritime dandelion; blooms yellow, on branching stems, at the top of the plant. Oh, well, I suppose if they *say* it's a lettuce –

When we got back to base, Ronald Lockley had arrived from Bardsey. He told me he'd cracked a rib in the rough crossing; but no matter! He also said that the function of the tube noses of fulmars, petrels, shearwaters and other albatrosses is probably to excrete salt water. They drink salt water, of course, and there is a steady saline drip from the tubes.

fulmars –

23RD JULY

To-day we visited Puffin Island, off the east coast of Llangoed. This was something of a privilege, for the island – perhaps a shade over half a mile long and 400 yards across – is a nature reserve, not to be visited without permission.

To me the greatest sight of the day was the kittiwakes (*Rissa tridactyla*). These birds, of the gull family, nest on ledges on sheer cliff-faces, and on this account feel instinctively secure against intruders. Consequently the young, when approached, simply stay put – neither they nor their parents have any inbred instinct to fly away. If something predatory – say, a great black-backed gull – comes to pick them off their ledge, there's nothing much they can do about it. But for the most part they're safe enough on their sheer faces.

Richard Arnold called me up onto a projecting bluff and invited me to look along to my left. On a ledge not twenty yards away, two pairs of kittiwakes were beside their young. Their heads, shoulders and upper parts were pure white, the feathers so close and smooth that one might imagine them made of marble: the wings and back pale grey, with black-tipped primaries. Their beaks were shorter and slimmer than those of herring gulls, dull yellow, with no red feeding-patch at the base; the legs black. The impression they gave, seen thus at close quarters, was of graceful, alert delicacy. The flat nests were made of seaweed, grass and mud. The black-and-grey chicks showed no alarm at all. Richard pointed out a black patch at the back of their heads. When two chicks squabble, the one who feels inferior ducks its head, exposing the black patch. The effect is to satisfy the antagonist's aggressive feelings and cause it to break off its attack. (I suggested calling this 'the Uncle patch'.)

~ kittiwakes
on ledge ~

Richard showed us a young shag, which he picked up and held. They have a webbed foot with two membranes between three ribs. The feet are very warm to the touch; they incubate their eggs with them. This shag, instead of pecking, gripped my thumb hard in its slightly serrated beak. I felt it just as it meant me to.

The lesser black-backed gull (*Larus fuscus*) differs from the greater (*Larus marinus*) in having yellow, not buff, legs and a back of a less intense black. They are also, of course, smaller. The two species sometimes interbreed, but the hybrid, Ronald Lockley tells me, seems not to be able to reproduce itself.

Later, we saw a bull and five or six cow grey seals on the rocks at the north-eastern extremity of the island. The cows, alarmed, dived into the sea, but the bull remained on the rocks placidly enough. He was patched black and grey, very large, with an elephantine nose.

High up on the cliff, among bracken, we unexpectedly found a red-breasted merganser's nest (*Mergus serrator*) with seven eggs. The hen flew off, and we could see it cruising about in the sea several hundred feet below us. Richard Arnold said he was amazed to find a red-breasted merganser's nest on top of a cliff, but Ronald said he'd come upon their nests on cliff-tops in the Faroes.

We found a garden tiger moth (*Arctia caja*) – most beautiful, the orange under-wings spotted dark blue, the head and shoulders thickly covered with dark-blue 'fur'.

Also, I happened on a beetle which I must identify later, for no one knew it. It was about as long as my top thumb-joint, with clubbed antennae; the black back barred with two broad orange stripes. I don't think it could fly.

Joke by John Guest: 'It's all right to kiss a nun now and then, but you mustn't get into the habit.'

24TH JULY

To-day we watched black guillemots. There are only four pairs breeding on Anglesey altogether. (We have several on Man, however.) From the cliff we watched ten of these birds 'loitering' in a flotilla on the calm sea below. This species doesn't migrate, apparently. In summer they are black, with white wing-patches, but in winter they become rather like a piebald pigeon. They're not really guillemots, being a different genus and no more related

~ black guillemot ~

to a common guillemot than to a puffin or a razorbill. Unlike the common guillemot, they can stand up!

In the afternoon, on Llyn Alaw, we saw a ruff and a reeve (male and female) – early migrant waders (*Philomachus pugnax*). Richard Arnold said that ruffs ringed in this country have been recovered south of the Sahara and in central Asia!

A lot of water plantain (*Alisma plantago-aquatica*) in bloom along the Llyn Alaw. Very attractive, with its white, three-petalled flowers.

25TH JULY

The course ended to-day, and in the afternoon Ronald Lockley, Stewart and I drove up to Chester. I brought away a souvenir in the form of two piddock-pierced stones, with which the beach of Puffin Island is covered. The outstanding characteristic of the shellfish called Pholadidae, or piddocks – fairly small bivalves – is their ability to bore into anything at all, including stone. To quote the *Penguin Nature Guide on Seashells*, 'By alternately contracting and expanding the anterior adductor muscles, the piddock twists and rocks its valves, which have scales and spines at the front. The resultant rasping effect enables it to bore a vertical, symmetrical hole in its chosen material. A piddock remains throughout its life in the tomb it has made for itself.' Two empty tombs in my pocket now. They are flattish stones, one about two inches and the other two and a half inches long. One has been pierced through three times; the other is pierced once, but also has three deep, semi-cylindrical, smooth grooves in its upper surface.

piddock
Stone –

26TH JULY

We walked round Chester on the walls. Buddleia in bloom and dark-red hollyhocks; heliotrope too. Perhaps the heavy day made it feel more autumnal than it really was. On the wall, Ronald parted from us to take the train for London.

While returning on the steam-packet to Man, Stewart and I saw guillemots, ringed plovers and several gannets flying not far from the ship.

That large, very yellow 'dandelion' (22nd July) certainly was *not* *Lactuca virosa*. The pictures in Fitter and Fitter and Keble Martin represent *Lactuca virosa* quite differently. It was probably *Sonchus arvensis* (so not particularly maritime.)

Another dull, overcast, humid day. I took Tetter out over Carraghan, down as far as St Luke's at East Baldwin and back by the Injebreck reservoir and Injebreck House. All very quiet, the river Glas down to a mere trickle. Fuchsia in bloom everywhere, and bell heather. At the south end of Injebreck reservoir I came upon a little grove of wild cherries, the fruit all red-and-yellow on the trees. I picked several, which were so ripe that they came off the stones when pulled. They were half-sweet, and very refreshing. Why haven't the birds had them, I wonder?

My orange-and-black beetle (23rd July) must have been *Necrophorus investigator*, of the family Silphidae, the burying beetles. All these sexton beetles have strongly clubbed antennae, which was the first thing I noticed about mine, after its orange stripes. They are attracted to carrion. A pair, having taken possession of a carcase, mate; and then bury the carcase (mouse, mole, etc.). Once that's done, the female excavates a small passage leading off from the burial chamber and lays her eggs there. Later, the young feed off the carcase. (Edgar Allan Poe?)

104

28TH JULY

Hot and thundery all day – oppressive. During my absence, Clif
Dadd has put a hundred golden orfe (*Leuciscus idus aureatus*) into
the lake, as well as a hundred koi carp. In the heat of the day you
can see them plainly from the library windows, idling in the
shallows along the shore. According to A. Laurence Wells (*The
Observer's Book of Freshwater Fishes of the British Isles*) golden orfe are
'the most popular of all pond fishes'. They grow very rapidly,
apparently, and are active in catching mosquitoes. I only trust that
that heron –

29TH JULY

Desperately hot, oppressive and thundery, with a coppery, molten
shine on the sea. I found the brookweed (*Samolus valerandi*) in
bloom at last, in a damp bank beside the path leading down to the
beach just north of Gob-ny-Deigan. 'Damp places near the sea.'
(Fitter.) I'd never seen brookweed until I came to the Island. It's
one of the Primulaceae. Now, I always go and look for it in late
July.

Rosamond's bonsai elm still thrives. I gave it a dash of bone-
meal to-day.

30TH JULY

Fine weather. This evening I had a walk up the sandy beach
between the Lhen trench and Blue Point. The air was full of terns
– mainly Little terns, but also some Common and at least one
Arctic (scarlet beak). More excitingly (for me, anyway – a bit
surfeited with terns!) I suddenly saw, quite close, what I now
believe was a bar-tailed godwit. It was a fairly large wader with a

longish beak, speckled brown back, the breast light-coloured but speckled faintly with ochre; legs dark. It ran true to form in being on a sandy, stony beach, well above the water-line. It was solitary, and this too is not improbable.

31ST JULY

I omitted to record, on 24th July, that when we were on the Llyn Alaw that evening, Richard Arnold observed a wader which he thought might be a pectoral sandpiper (*Calidris melanotos*). This bird breeds in north-east Siberia and northern North America, and is not normally seen in the British Isles. Nevertheless, it seems that a few occasionally wander here. Naturally, Richard was wary about identifying it.

To-day I've received a letter from him, in which he says 'The mystery wader really *was* a pectoral sandpiper from North America. An average of some thirty turn up each year in the British Isles. First I've seen, though. I went out on 26th July, and watched it at sixty yards on the ground and in flight. No doubt. I have sent in the record with a full field description.' (I.e. to the R.S.P.B.)

August

1ST AUGUST

Pat and Joan Benner arrived for a few days. They're great walkers, bird-watchers and wild-flower enthusiasts. This afternoon we walked on the sandy beach near Blue Point, and just about everything – or so it seemed – turned out for them. We saw four kinds of tern – Little, Common, Arctic and Sandwich. (Sandwich with yellow tip to beak.) Several gannets off shore, and no fewer than three seals visible off shore simultaneously.

Wild flowers included the sea-rocket – pink-flowered, fleshy, maritime crucifer (*Cakile maritima*) – common enough, of course, on sandy beaches at this time of year; and, when we turned inland, onto the waste meadows called the Ayres, the soft-headed, dusty pale-pink hare's-foot clover (*Trifolium arvense*) – longish, oval flower-heads bunched all over a tight, neat plant. The perennial centaury, too (*Centaurium scilloides*), was flowering thickly. (And I mean thickly – an extensive, rose-pink patch as big as a service court on a lawn tennis court.)

2ND AUGUST

Clif Dadd called this morning to see how the lake was getting on, and pointed out to me that (a) the golden orfe and koi carp are

hare's-foot
clover

thriving and (b) there is quite a bit of *Callitriche* – starwort – growing in the water. This seemed to please him. I consulted Fitter and Fitter. 'Callitriche. Water starwort. A difficult group, leaf shape varying with presence or depth of water, and the ripe fruit needed for sure identification often hard to find. Annuals/perennials, partly submerged or on wet mud.' Do I want Callitrichaceae? We'll see, no doubt.

Out on the Peel cliffs this afternoon, with Pat, Joan and Stewart. The guillemots and razorbills are all gone, but there were plenty of puffins; and just a few kittiwakes still nesting. Also, a flotilla of black guillemots cruising round, to the Benners' great delight.

It came on to rain pretty heavily, and in the thick of this rain we saw, quite close to, a large bird, a raptor, black (blacker because of the rain, I dare say) with a conspicuous white bar at the base of the tail. I believe it to have been a female hen harrier (*Circus cyaneus*).

Small copper

3RD AUGUST

I took Pat and Joan down to the Chasms this afternoon. There were several choughs (*Pyrrhocorax pyrrhocorax*) at the base of the cliff. Just one or two fulmars, but almost all gone now; nor could we see any chicks on the ledges. (Parent fulmars desert their single chick about now. It remains on the nesting-ledge for about a week, living off its fat, until finally it takes the plunge and flies off on its own.)

Saw several red admirals; and a beautiful small copper (*Lycaena phlaeas*) poised on some yarrow, its colouring and markings very vivid and distinct: the upper wings with a narrow, white outer

choughs

border, then inside that a broader, dark border, then the black-spotted, ochreous colouring. The lower wings were narrowly edged white, then orange within that, then the rest of the wing dark, smoky brown.

The Dadds Show garden –

4TH AUGUST

This morning I took Pat and Joan over to see Clif's professional show gardens at Glen Roy, on the other side of the Island. While walking along one of the upper paths, well above the stream, we (all four of us) saw a large tortoiseshell butterfly (*Nymphalis polychloros*) sunning itself on a patch of grass beside the path. It flew off with a rapid, flickering, twisting flight, similar to that of a painted lady. Large tortoiseshells are uncommon nowadays. (The butterfly doesn't emerge from the chrysalis until July or August.)

Later, I saw the orange hawkweed (*Pilosella aurantiacum*) in bloom by the roadside. First I've seen this year, though Fitter and Fitter give the blooming period as June onwards. This flower is not in Keble Martin at all! Inexplicable, for it's common. Jove nodding and how!

Pat and Joan left this evening.

5TH AUGUST

Watched birds on the cliffs south of Peel Castle. The young kittiwakes, now flown and frequenting the cliffs on their own account, were very striking, seen from above. Their white wings are edged entirely round with black, reminding me of the visiting cards that used to be left by ladies in mourning when I was a small boy more than fifty years ago. Their heads, also, are black-and-white – unusual and conspicuous marking.

6TH AUGUST

As dusk was falling this evening I was talking to Juliet on the telephone when all of a sudden, looking out of the library window, I saw the great, undulating, black wings of a heron coming in low over the lake. Talk about 'Janet, donkeys!' I was out there in my carpet slippers in ten seconds. The heron had alighted all right; but it took off again at my urgent instigation. I can see that my troubles as a lake-owner are just beginning.

7TH AUGUST

Pouring rain all day: but a fine display of little birds in the trees and bushes. There must have been a hatch of some sort of fly or bug, to attract so many. I saw blue tits, coal tits, a goldcrest and – very attractive, these – four or five young, recently flown willow warblers. (I suppose they *were* willow warblers and not chiff-chaffs. They had the dark bar across the eye.) Their behaviour was very much that of warblers, graceful, flickering and restless. All had vividly yellow underparts. This is a characteristic of the young bird: as they get older they get paler.

Ronald Lockley, on the telephone, confirms that the raptor seen on the cliff on 2nd August sounded to him like a female hen harrier.

A local name both in Wiltshire and in Yorkshire for the valerian is 'cat's love', and also 'cat-trail' (Geoffrey Grigson, *The Englishman's Flora*).

I tried some dried roots of common valerian on our cat. (See entry for 19th June.) He was very enthusiastic for about a minute, sniffing and biting like mad, but then lost interest, and has shown none since.

I note with interest the following lines from the Milleres Tale in *The Canterbury Tales*. Chaucer is describing the room in his house which the Miller let to that engaging rascal, hende Nicholas.

> 'A chambre hadde he in that hostelrye
> Allone, with-outen any companye,

> Ful fetisly y-dight with herbes swote;
> And he him-self as swete as is the rote
> Of licorys, or any cetewale.'

'Cetewale' is given in the glossary as 'valerian'. Now, might this not be an early form of 'caterwaul', the origin of which is given in my *Shorter Oxford English Dictionary* as Middle English, with an addendum, 'The relation between the many forms [of the word] is not clear'? It is interesting that the Dictionary gives two meanings of the word; first, to make the noise proper to cats at rutting time, and secondly, to be in heat; to behave lasciviously. Either way, this all seems quite appropriate to hende Nicholas and to the Milleres Tale.

8TH AUGUST

The disused railway cutting is full of brambles covered with pink flowers; and now the green berries are forming as the petals disappear.

9TH AUGUST

More rain; but they'll be harvesting soon, I suppose. Oats and barley both look ripe. Crossed to London this evening, to take Julie and Ros. to Glyndebourne to-morrow. The garden below their flat looks as well kept and flourishing as usual. Hostas in pale-mauve bloom, but the hollyhocks are only just coming into flower.

10TH AUGUST

To Glyndebourne, with Julie and Ros., to see Elizabeth Harwood as the Feldmarschallin in *Rosenkavalier*. (Haitink conducting.) A splendid performance. The weather was fine – indeed, it was a perfect evening for Glyndebourne. We walked by the lake and admired the beds of white water-lilies (*Nymphaea alba*) in bloom. The mulberries were falling or else fallen from the big, old tree at the top of the lawn in the corner of the wall, and we ate some. The flower-beds contained, as usual, several unusual things, the names of which I didn't know. I suppose if they labelled them it would be rather out of keeping with the informal, 'private garden' atmosphere; but it would be nice to be able to identify some of these shrubs and herbaceous flowers that one hasn't seen before.

11TH AUGUST

On my way to dinner with John Guest, who lives between Victoria and Sloane Square, I was delighted, as I walked along, by the great profusion of flowers in window-boxes and hanging baskets. I noted the following, though I don't think the list's exhaustive: lobelia, nasturtium, alyssum, pelargonium, *Phlox drummondii*, several unusual shades of petunia, several kinds of ivy, double marigolds, fuchsia, plumbago, geraniums, marguerite daisies, coleus, golden rod, michaelmas daisies, delphiniums and nicotianas.

13TH AUGUST

This evening I met Ronald Lockley for dinner at the house of an old friend of his, Mrs Bowman, who lives in the neighbourhood of Camden Town/Regent's Park. In her charming little 'courtyard' garden I saw a very unusual and plainly exotic tree. It had large, lanceolate, glaucous leaves – as long as my hand or longer – and a very 'open' style of growth, both branches and leaves relatively wide apart. Mrs Bowman told me it was a loquat; she had brought a seed back from Turkey some years ago. It had never fruited, however: probably, she thought, because it couldn't get cross-fertilization. This is an entirely new one on me. It's not mentioned in Alan Mitchell's *Field Guide to the Trees of Britain and Northern Europe*.

She also had a beautiful contorted willow (*Salix matsudana* 'Tortuosa') which Mitchell describes as 'a cultivar of a very rare species, now quite commonly planted'. 'Crisped and curled boat-shaped leaves.' I'd like to have one of these myself; and in fact I will: on the island in the lake.

14TH AUGUST

Glad to get back home to-day.

15TH AUGUST

Walking along the Switchback lane this afternoon, I saw half a dozen swallows lined up on a telegraph wire, making short, tentative flights and returning. There certainly has been a good deal of rain and mist lately, but mid-August seems a bit early. Don't go yet!

16TH AUGUST

A sea-fret, like cotton-wool, has hung close about the house all day, blotting out the half-mile between here and the sea. It lifted at evening, and later we had a beautifully clear, starlit night. Strolling out about midnight, I watched Aquila moving across the ecliptic, with the Dolphin following. There wasn't a cloud in the sky, and all the constellations were clear to be seen – Pegasus in the east and Arcturus in the west.

There were three female mallard on the lake at nightfall. The maroon water-lilies Clif planted are in bud and should bloom within the week.

17TH AUGUST

There are still plenty of terns along the beach at Blue Point. Also a good many gannets out at sea: they never approach the beach. Saw a seal fairly close in. There were a lot of pied wagtails running about on the beach. I suppose they're in passage south.

In the garden this evening I came upon a fine plant of *Fumaria capreolata*, the ramping fumitory. This is much bigger than the common fumitory; a handsome, trailing plant, with white flowers tipped – in this case – almost black.

ramping fumitory –

18TH AUGUST

Something rather interesting happened this afternoon. I was coming down across the tract of moor north-east of the Guthrie memorial, which is in effect the lower northern slope of North Barrule, above Glen Auldyn. Some little distance off, a fairly large bird appeared, flying up over the heather from below. It was flying in a curiously clumsy, sort of loutish way, making a short flight and then stopping and hanging around for a minute or so before making another. Two smaller birds were flying behind it, making a fuss, calling and appearing perturbed. At first I thought it was a kestrel, but as it came closer I saw that in fact it was a young cuckoo. The other two birds were meadow pipits. This rather macabre little group went blundering on their way and eventually all disappeared together over the North Barrule ridge.

The fostered cuckoo was evidently flying off on its migration – late, too, I'd think – and the parent pipits were plainly wondering what was going on. The ways of Nature are strange at times. It had no doubt killed the meadow pipits' brood by kicking them out of the nest, and now they were upset because it was leaving them.

pied wagtails on the beach —

19TH AUGUST

In the disused railway cutting, under the bridge carrying the lane between East Lhergy Dhoo Farm and Ballagyr, there is a great mass of bindweed with very large, pink flowers with narrow, white stripes. This has puzzled me for some little while past, and to-day I tore out a length and brought it back.

It throws an interesting light on the wild-flower books in popular use, and is a triumph for Fitter, Fitter and Blamey. I will expound. First, Fitch and Smith's *Illustrations of the British Flora* illustrates only three bindweeds. They call them all '*Convolvulus*': the lesser (*arvensis*), the larger (*sepium*) and the maritime (*soldanella*). This wasn't any of those. Keble Martin gives four, one of which he doesn't illustrate. *He* calls them *Calystegia* – *sepium, soldanella* and *sylvatica*, plus *Convolvulus arvensis*. *Sylvatica*'s the one he doesn't illustrate, and he says nothing as to the colour of its blooms, leaving one to infer that they are invariably white, like *sepium*, which he *does* illustrate (as white – the hooded bindweed, as my father used to call it) and which precedes *sylvatica* in his text.

Finally, Fitter and Fitter. They give five bindweeds (the extra one being *Convolvulus pulchra*, 'widely naturalized, probably of garden origin'). Of *Calystegia sepium* they say: 'Flowers white, rarely pink . . . Two large but not overlapping sepal-like bracts enclosing the five narrower sepals.' Of *Calystegia sylvatica* they say: 'Has larger flowers, occasionally pink or pink-striped, and larger, almost inflated overlapping bracts, hiding the sepals. Often commoner in and around human settlements.' (They don't say why.) I looked at my specimen, with its pink, white-striped flowers, and there were the two overlapping bracts, large as life, hiding the sepals. So that's that – *Convolvulus sylvatica*, the great bindweed, the less common, pink, white-striped variety, is blooming in the disused railway cutting.

(But Fitter and Fitter say 'pink-striped' [*sic*] and these flowers are predominantly pink, with narrow white stripes. Oh, well.)

20TH AUGUST

Tetter and I, off for a walk this evening, accepted a lift from Janice as far as Ballig. On the way, along the Switchback, we encountered a polecat-ferret. It took a good, steady look at the car and then sauntered into the grass verge. Janice, though a Manx girl, had never happened on one before.

These polecat-ferrets are the Island's largest – indeed, almost its only – wild mammalian predator. They are fairly big for a British wild animal – a shade smaller than a medium-sized cat – and in colour vary a good deal, although they always have an admixture of dark or smoke-coloured fur. Some are cream-coloured, like a ferret, with smoky extremities. Others, like this one to-night, are sort of tawny, with black extremities and smoky masks, etc. The polecat-ferrets were introduced for rabbiting during the last century and some escaped and went feral. To-day there are plenty. They are commonest in the northern hill area, but we get quite a few round here, in the central west. They live mostly on rabbits, rats, voles, mice, etc., but on occasion and opportunity are not above a chicken run or a rubbish-bin. They are said to be fierce when cornered. It is interesting that they are only half-afraid of man. If you meet one up on the moors, as I have now and then while walking, he will stand his ground and watch you. He keeps his distance, but he doesn't turn and run, like a true wild animal. You sometimes see them dead on the road – for the same reason, perhaps.

Another interesting ornithological incident to-day. I was descending one of the rather steep, narrow, half-wooded glens (or 'brooghs', to use the Manx word) which break up the lower north-west slope of Slieau Whallian. I was on a narrow track and half-hidden in tall fern well up to my waist, when I became aware of a corvine of some kind, flying low along the length of the broogh ahead. It turned and came back. It was a chough. It passed within a few feet of my head, giving its characteristic, low, 'cacking' cry. Then it turned again. No one, really, can ever have seen a chough to much better advantage: the red legs; red, down-curved beak; separated primaries; glossy plumage, the darkest possible blue – some would say black, but strong light shows the midnight blue. What it was doing I don't know. Perhaps, deep in that fern, I didn't register as a human being. It flew back and forth past me repeatedly – I could have touched it – until, dropping down towards the bed of the stream below, it disappeared among the trees.

This broogh is about a mile and a half from the nearest sea as the chough flies.

Night falls early now. It's dark by half past nine.

22ND AUGUST

The hen harrier – or *a* hen harrier, anyway – was over my library windows at eleven o'clock this morning. I was scribbling away when I half-noticed a kind of alteration in the behaviour of the swallows darting about outside. The next moment, not thirty feet above the window I was looking out of, appeared the dark hawk-shape, with the white bar at the base of the tail. It half-hovered, maintaining a level height, but moving about over an area perhaps fifty yards square. Finally it flew off inland, up the hill.

Julie and Peter arrived this evening, for three days.

23RD AUGUST

This was a perfect August day – about the first we've had. Hot, cloudless sunshine and just a light breeze. Driving over to Ballaugh this morning, I saw the first wheat harvest under way.

In the afternoon Julie, Peter and I walked on the beach near Blue Point. There were just a few terns – Little, and Common. Otherwise only oyster-catchers, ringed plovers, gulls and shags.

24TH AUGUST

This morning (Sunday), driving to Holy Communion at Ballaugh with Elizabeth, I noticed a great black-backed gull gliding above and to the left of the car, with which it was keeping pace. The car was going at about thirty-eight miles per hour, and the gull was not over-exerting itself.

25TH AUGUST

Julie and Peter returned to London this evening.

There was a very large spider, perhaps one and a half inches in diameter, leg to leg, on the library floor this evening – another sign of approaching autumn, I'd say. Spiders, not being insects, don't appear in books on insects. I tried the *Encyclopaedia Brit.* on spiders, then on 'Arachnida'. Too difficult for me, I fear, though good stuff.

I've never understood some people's phobia of spiders. They can't bite or sting, and they're afraid of you, so what's the problem? Anyway, this particular spider disappeared before Janice could encounter him. Just as well for her.

26TH AUGUST

There are a great many chaffinches in the garden – flocks. The reason is that it isn't really a garden (yet), but wild. Just now, the wild grasses are all in seed, to say nothing of the ragwort, burdock, nipplewort, thistles, etc. Finches are seed-eaters. I watched a cock chaffinch going methodically over a burdock, while above him a coal tit did the same for a thorn tree. The tit was after insects, I suppose.

27TH AUGUST

A splendid walk in the fine weather: starting from the Peel–Douglas road, up the Greeba (about forty-five minutes), then along the ridge, down by Glen Helen and so home. On the Greeba I saw eight ravens strung out over about half a mile, and three kestrels.

The ling (*Calluna vulgaris*), which blooms later than either the bell heather or the cross-leaved heath, is in full bloom just now. It imparts to the hills and moors what John Clare called a 'saddened' (by which he meant 'toned-down, dull' – a woollen-trade term), dusty mauve. As one walks through it, one's boots kick up a light, cloudy pollen.

The robins have begun their sharp, autumnal twitterings along the edges of the brake; staking out autumn territory already.

Ate three ripe blackberries off a bush this afternoon.

Seed pods of the
Crinodendron bush -

mermaid's purse —

28TH AUGUST

My Brack-a-Broom lane, cottage garden friend has given me several seed-pods off his *Crinodendron* bush. The seed-pods are pendent and green, like little lanterns, each containing a great many white seeds. These, I'm advised, should be planted while still moist and white – not dried first.

29TH AUGUST

Elizabeth and I walked on the cliffs at Orrisdale. I cannot identify the eyebright there. Keble Martin lists twenty eyebrights, but he depicts only seven, none of which it is. It is most like *Euphrasia brevipila*, but does not branch.

On the beach, Elizabeth found a small moss-agate and a 'mermaid's purse' – an egg-case of the greater spotted dogfish. Also some rather attractive bits of *Alcyonidia* – sponge-like fragments, lobed and 'fingered', about as big as the top joint of one's thumb. They are coloured sort of ginger, and when dried become rubbery, with a pleasantly soft, velvety surface-texture.

30TH AUGUST

At this time of year the foliage of the burnet rose gradually changes from green to a kind of dark olive-bronze. The seed-pods, which are perhaps half as big as one's little finger-nail, are a regular, pointed ovoid in shape (brandy-bottle shaped), and glossy black, with a hint of red when seen in a strong light.

This is the time of year when I always enjoy seeing the purple clematis on porches and trellises. Of course, it's a marvellous time of year for all sorts of brilliantly coloured flowers, what with dahlias, begonias, antirrhinums, asters, phlox and the like: but there's no colour to match that of a purple clematis against a wall.

31ST AUGUST

The bush of Spiraea (*Spiraea japonica*) in the garden down by the Tynwald Mills, identified for me by Clif in the spring, when it was showing nothing but thin, cream- and maroon-tinged leaves, is now covered with flat umbels of dark-red inflorescence, anything from two and a half inches to half an inch in diameter.

September

1ST SEPTEMBER

Out on the Switchback this afternoon with Tetter, I saw a raven
flying along with something in its beak. Through binoculars this
was revealed as a dead mouse (or a young rat, I hope). The raven
alighted not far off and put the mouse down on the grass. However,
in about half a minute it picked it up again and once more took to
the air. It was then pursued by a herring gull which followed it,
screaming aggressively. The gull did not attack, and I was surprised
that it adopted this aggressive behaviour with a raven. I suppose it
was merely a conditioned reflex on seeing another bird with a
large morsel of food. After all, gulls treat each other like that all
the time.

Found in a meadow a tiny, blue, five-petalled flower with five
pointed sepals and minute, sky-blue stamens tightly together. It
can only be a flax, so I suppose it must be *Linum bienne*: but it
doesn't look much like the pictures. D. E. Allen, *Flowering Plants
of the Isle of Man*, includes both *Linum bienne* and *catharticum*, and
also *Radida linoides*. This one I found has linear, alternate leaves,
the main stalk three inches long and very thin: flowers a strong,
clear blue. (Keble Martin describes the flowers of *bienne* as 'very
pale mauve'.) I'm not altogether satisfied that my flower was *Linum
bienne*, but can't suggest anything else.

2ND SEPTEMBER

The farmer at Ballagyr told me to-day that he never reckoned to
harvest before September.

I doubt the blackberries in the railway cutting will be much
good. Few are ripe yet, and I don't think they'll have enough sun
to give them flavour before colder weather starts.

4TH SEPTEMBER

In Douglas for attention to the car, I had a while to wait, so walked
in the sea-front gardens. The flower-beds were everything that
they ought to be – a splendid show, well kept. Dwarf dahlias,
canna lilies, a bed of purply-blue verbenas; stocks, petunias,
mesembrianthemums, penstemons, Dutch marigolds, antirrhinums, gladioli, pinks, standard fuchsias, alyssum, ageratum, lobelias,
asters, larkspur, a cultivated bugloss and a kind of borage,
nicotianas, everlasting daisies (pyrethrum?) and some bedded-out
geraniums. I don't know that they'd really omitted much!

Walking along the disused railway line with Claire Wrench, at the site of the Poortown halt we came upon a fine whitebeam which I've never noticed before. Heavy clusters of berries; some still green, some partly turned, some bright red – all in the same cluster. 'Seldom numerous or conspicuous for long,' says Alan Mitchell, 'soon eaten by birds.' I ate one. It was tart and slightly sweet – but mealy and not crisp enough. Richard Mabey (*Food for Free*) says: 'The berries are edible as soon as they begin to go rotten, like medlars. John Evelyn found them "not unpleasant" and recommended them in a concoction with wine and honey.' He can keep them for me.

George Wedd and Joan arrived to stay for three days; Julie and Peter for two.

8TH SEPTEMBER

A nice feature of the Island, I always think, are Manx gateposts. They are about five feet high and two and a half feet square, made of stone and/or brick, roughly mortared. On top is a square coping, with four gently sloping, triangular sides meeting in a blunt point. The attraction of these great bollards of rough masonry is what you find growing in the interstices: scurvy-grass, sea spleenwort, all sorts of lichen but especially the decorative ones like *Caloplaca citrina* and *Xanthoria parietina*; valerian, ivy-leaved toadflax; ragwort, of course (where *won't* it grow?) and many other mural plants. Ubiquitous, casual wall-gardens: perhaps one might try planting a few things in them deliberately?

George and Joan left this evening.

9TH SEPTEMBER

Many fields have been cut and carried now. Barley is left later than wheat. I've been looking among the stubble for weeds of harvest. I've always wanted to find a blue pimpernel (*Anagallis foemina*) but never have. My favourite weed of harvest – one you don't often find – is Fluellen (*Kickxia elatine*). The vivid purple and yellow together in the same bloom delight me.

Incidentally, where did Shakespeare get the name 'Fluellen'? The word isn't in the dictionary; nor is it a place-name in my atlas of the British Isles. Dover Wilson on *Henry V* offers no suggestions. Geoffrey Grigson, *The Englishman's Flora*, doesn't even mention the flower. Llewellyn, perhaps?

10TH SEPTEMBER

This afternoon I came upon a devil's coach-horse running about. I took him on my hand, whereupon he cocked up his rear-end in the approved manner. Coleoptera: a rove beetle of the Staphylinidae. To be specific, this chap was *Ocypus olens*. There are nearly

1,000 species of rove beetles in Britain, says Michael Chinery. The devil's coach-horse can fly well, having large hind wings, though only short *elytra* (the hard and horny front wings). He is a predator on fly larvae, etc.

11TH SEPTEMBER

Out in the Ballaglass Glen area this afternoon, I came upon a house by the stream with a forecourt paved with old flagstones. Between these was growing in profusion a small, yellow-blooming plant with linear leaves like grass-blades: the bloom small – rather smaller than a buttercup, but not dissimilar in shape and appearance. I guessed, however, that it was probably of the iris family. Later, Clif confirmed me. It is *Sisyrinchium* – new to me. It made those flagstones look beautiful. I must get some for the garden. 'Easy enough to grow,' says Clif. The blooms close at night in a very charming way.

12TH SEPTEMBER

Earwig time! They come dropping out of everything – vegetables, dahlias – even the newspaper this morning. Personally, I like an earwig. They do no harm. 'Dermapteza are a very small order, with only about 1,000 known species, and the British earwig fauna is very meagre indeed, only two species being at all common.'

(Chinery.) As far north as this, earwigs are apparently at the limit of their range. They are nocturnal, and they winter in the soil. The British two, *Forficula auricularia* and *Labia minor*, can tolerate quite a bit of cold. 'They seem to like to feel their bodies in contact with something when at rest.' This, no doubt, is why they get into things and fall out of them when disturbed. Michael Chinery goes on: 'The wings are folded very elaborately . . . If you try to unfold the wings . . . you will realize just how elaborately. There are about forty thicknesses of each wing when completely folded.' *Forficula can* fly, but doesn't, much. 'One might be tempted to think that he finds it too much trouble to get his wings out and then put them away again.' I know that feeling.

14TH SEPTEMBER

On the edge of a sheltered garden along a lane I came upon a holly-like bush. Indeed, the leaves were indistinguishable from those of ordinary holly. This shrub was bearing thinly tubular, red flowers with yellow tips, each about an inch and a quarter long. They had no scent and were hirsute – well, sort of 'furry'. This turns out to be *Desfontainea spinosa*, one of the Palaliaceae, originating in the western regions of South America – the Andes to the Straits of Magellan. I think I ought to install one of these, too, in the garden. If it can tolerate the area of the Straits of Magellan, it *must* be hardy; and the flowers are most attractive.

15TH SEPTEMBER

My friend from Denmark, Helgi Jonsson, is here for a week. Helgi loves the Island, on account of the hills, the tidal sea and the noisy, fast-flowing streams: on Sjælland they have none of these things. This afternoon, the tops being misty, he suggested a beach walk, so we went along below Orrisdale. Nothing but curlews, oyster-catchers and ringed plovers, though I *may* have seen a tern, I think.

17TH SEPTEMBER

Anniversary of Arnhem. Paddy Kavanagh; Thompson; Daniels; Sergeant Walsh. May they rest in peace.

Almighty God, we humbly thank Thee for the courage and devotion to duty of all members of the 1st Airborne Division, who died to save us from evil, tyranny and oppression. Grant that their supreme sacrifice may not have been in vain, and that we may never forget what they did for us and always honour them in our hearts. And if it be Thy will, grant that they and we may meet in Thy heavenly kingdom, with Jesus Christ Our Lord. Amen.

Helgi and I took out a saw and knife and severed the ivy infesting some of the bigger ash trees along the Switchback. Ash is ivy's commonest victim. There are several ashes round here I'd like to rescue.

19TH SEPTEMBER

Helgi, Janice and I planned to walk from Cronk ny Arrey Laa (a western mountain) to Niarbyl and back, but just as we reached the Cronk in the car it began to rain very heavily. This caused us to lose a good three-quarters of an hour, so we abandoned our original idea and went down to the Manx folk museum at Cregneish. Helgi was delighted with the four-horned Loghtan ram, and took several photographs. Then we walked to Spanish Head (where there *may* be an Armada galleon sunk – and then again there may not). I had never before done this short but very beautiful walk. It's well worth-while – a path along high cliffs of Manx slate above a clear, deep sea, with a view across to the Calf (the island at the south-westerly foot of the Island itself). We finished Helgi's outing by taking him to see the nearby Meall stone circle, a multiple stone burial-site, *circa* 1800 B.C.

20TH SEPTEMBER

Out walking this afternoon, poor Stewart met with an unlucky accident. Helgi, Janice, Stewart and I had set out to walk over the summit of Cronk ny Arrey Laa, down the steep west face to the little *keeill* (ruined chapel) at the foot, thence to Niarbyl and back by way of the footpath that runs near a farmhouse called Eary Cushlan. From the summit of the Cronk, Stewart chose a line down the west face which quite honestly I thought was a bit too steep. However, I couldn't insist on abandoning it, so down we went. Soon the going became very steep – in places almost sheer. The rocks were wet and slippery, but between them were patches of heather and grass. Suddenly Stewart, who was about thirty yards below and ahead of us, cried out, slithered and vanished. Janice was admirable. She remained completely level-headed and self-controlled. Stewart called up, from thirty or forty feet below, that he was more-or-less all right, but battered. Soon we saw him emerge into the heather and continue down towards the path running parallel to the sea along the mountain's foot. We had to go round quite a long way to continue our descent and join him. When we'd all joined up again, Stewart told us he thought he'd damaged his hand. We returned round the north side of the mountain via Eary Cushlan as soon as we could. As Helgi said, thank goodness he hadn't broken a limb or knocked himself unconscious, for his evacuation from so remote a spot would have been awkward.

21ST SEPTEMBER

Helgi left this afternoon.

Stewart went to the hospital this morning, where they X-rayed him and strapped him up. He has cracked two bones in his right hand. (He's left-handed, which is a slight consolation.) You'd never have guessed he was injured, from his demeanour at dinner last night. Very stalwart bloke, Stewart – *quocunque jeceris stabit.* (Motto of the Isle of Man.)

A great deal of swallow and martin activity above the fields this afternoon. They're always more active shortly before they go. By the time I get back from Australia on 9th October they'll all be gone.

22ND SEPTEMBER

At last I've found something wrong in the perfect cottage garden down Brack-a-Broom lane! In the September sunshine this afternoon, with the dahlias glowing and all the brassicas doing well, the apple tree (not a big one, but fruiting heavily) was a solid mass of wasps – black with them. A horrible sight! The nest must be near by. It ought to be poisoned, but I dare say tracking it down (probably on someone else's land) is too much of a job for my friend, who's no longer young.

Crossed to London in the evening.

23RD SEPTEMBER

In London. The horse chestnut leaves are all turned – some yellow, some flame-coloured, many just dull brown.

25TH SEPTEMBER

Elizabeth and I spent a little while at St Paul's Cathedral this morning. In Godliman Street, leading from Queen Victoria Street up to St Paul's, are four willow trees. I wonder what kind they are?

Without a book I was unable to tell. It's delightful to see a row of four willows in central London. I always enjoy seeing the enormous ailanthus trees ('tree of heaven', *Ailanthus altissima*) growing along the south side of St Paul's. They must each be fifty or sixty feet high, and clearly like their situation. At the moment the great, pinnate leaves are still green – don't even look like turning, let alone falling.

In St James's Park, patches of autumn crocus (*Colchicum speciosum autumnale*, I think) both purple and white (or white flushed pale mauve).

26TH SEPTEMBER

At 10 p.m. Julie and I took off from Heathrow for Melbourne and my promotional tour of Australia.

28TH SEPTEMBER

Early morning. Over central Australia. We've now been flying for twenty-three hours, but as you lose (or gain?) nine hours on the trip, it's now six o'clock on the morning of Sunday the 28th. Flying over southern India yesterday morning was a stirring experience – looking down, between light patches of cloud, from nearly 40,000 feet, at just-discernible villages and green-and-brown fields. London to the Persian Gulf in six and a half hours, and only another eight hours on to Singapore. Whatever would Dr Johnson have said? ('Sir, I know not why a man should hold it such a marvel merely to out-pace the clock. What virtue lies in this, unless the traveller possess some discernment?' BOSWELL. 'But, sir, the air-hostesses are mighty comely and agreeable.' JOHNSON. 'Sir, this is nothing to the purpose.')

Nightfall found us crossing the Timor Sea. As I write now, the sun is rising over central Australia – a magnificent sight. An hour ago the clear night sky was bright with southern hemisphere stars (which I couldn't identify). Half an hour later the east became a long band of dark, glowing ochre. Up through this came the sun, first turning it to crimson, then dispersing it altogether. Now the east is so bright that there's no looking at it. Down below is nothing but brown, irregularly ribbed desert. *Benedicite, omnia opera Domini!* In one and a quarter hours we shall land at Sydney; then on to Melbourne.

Later: A brilliant spring morning. Snow-covered mountains between Sydney and Melbourne! At their foot a lake, a meandering river and a broad, green plain.

Later: Returning late to our hotel to-night, I was astonished to hear, from about a hundred yards away, the rich, whistling, melodious calls of a multitude of birds. They sounded rather like blackbirds – or even nightingales – very full and clear. It was, of course, night; and I could only suppose that this must be some sort of tape-recording. But why? I went in search. Across the road, about a hundred yards away, stood the Parliament Building, a majestic, colonnaded, nineteenth-century job, with a floodlit portico at the top of a flight of steps. My birds were roosting in flocks under the floodlit portico, just as our London starlings do. The floodlighting was stimulating them. I approached the young policeman on duty.

'What sort of birds are those, can you tell me?'

'I couldn't say.' (Nutty Pom!)

'Do they go on like that all night?'

'Off and on, yes.'

Indian mynahs? They're about the right size, and have white bars on the body: a bit like a small, brown moorhen to look at.

It's now midnight, my room is fifty yards away, the window is open and they're entirely silent, though the floodlighting is still on.

29TH SEPTEMBER (*Monday*)

Woke at half past five to hear the putative mynahs whistling and calling. I had a look out of the window. What I believe to have been Venus was 'a brilliant object' in a clear, eastern, spring sky, shining close beside the three spires of the cathedral. Melbourne is a quiet city.

I wish I knew the names of more Australian trees. Julie Steiner, our charming publicity girl, says she'll get me books. I need one for birds and one for flowers. Must try and get one for trees, too.

30TH SEPTEMBER

This afternoon, being photographed for the press in a place called Fitzroy Gardens, Julie and I found ourselves in an avenue of Moreton Bay figs. These are huge, spreading trees, their multiple trunks pale grey like beeches, but the bark a little rougher. (*Ficus*

macrophylla: I've got a book now!) The leaves are dark green and laurel-like in shape. The avenue is beautifully cool and shady. (The sun's very hot.) The trees are bearing green figs, which turn black and squashy as they ripen and fall. You *could* eat them, I suppose, at a pinch, but when opened they seem all seeds.

The Australian fig and banyan family (Moraceae) look and sound wonderful in the book. *Ficus lyrata*, the banjo fig (leaves like banjos). The variegated India rubber plant (*Ficus elastica variegata*). *Ficus rubiginosa* (the Port Jackson fig). *Ficus religiosa*, the sacred fig or Bo tree (under which the Buddha received enlightenment). *Ficus benjamina*, the weeping banyan. *Ficus retusa*, the Chinese banyan. (As Mr Pooter would say, I've *figured* them out.) I only wish we had longer here.

The roosting birds I tackled again last night with binoculars, but still couldn't really be sure. They behave like starlings, and they *look* like starlings, too. However, there are only two things they can be. First, the English starling, *Sturnus vulgaris*, or else the Indian mynah, *Acridotheres tristis*, which *is* a starling. They were not moving much last night, and I couldn't really see them plainly.

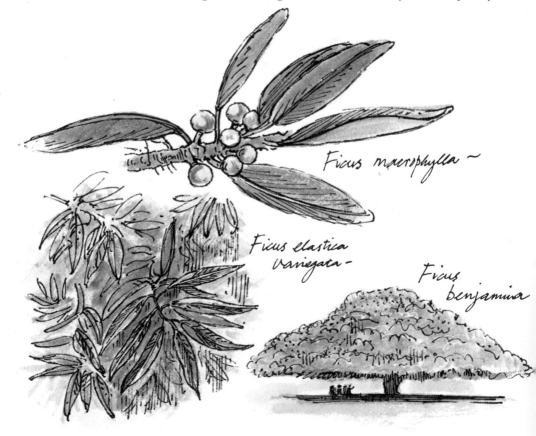

Ficus macrophylla ~

Ficus elastica
variegata ~

Ficus
benjamina

October

Malurus cyaneus —

Bauhinia blakeana

Erythrina caffra

Callistemon citrinus

1ST OCTOBER

I've got it! They are *mostly* mynahs, but among them are groups of starlings. This accounts for everything.

Early this morning went for a walk in the Fitzroy Gardens. Talking to a girl gardener, I learned that the staff come on duty at 7.30 a.m. The idea is to have the gardens fresh and pleasant 'by the time people want to start using them'. The lawns and flower-beds were hosed and sparkling; blackbirds and thrushes running and hopping over the grass: a perfect spring morning. Coral trees (*Erythrina* – er – *speciosa*, I think, but they could have been *caffra*) in brilliant scarlet bloom, each cluster big as a human fist, flowering on the bare bough before the unfolding of the heart-shaped leaves. The bark is silvery-grey. I've seen this beautiful tree before, in Los Angeles. Speaking of scarlet bloom, there were Bottle-brushes, too (*Callistemon citrinus*).

I saw a female blackbird with a beakful of lawn-mowing cuttings – nest-building, no doubt. It disappeared round a grove of red and white camellias. The following were in bloom: weigela, azalea, hellebore, a big orange geum, pansies and polyanthus; big *bushes* of salvia, three feet high; bluebells, aquilegias, myosotis; white, scented jasmine trained against a fence; viburnum, hibiscus. 'Haw! Haw!' said Mr Jorrocks. 'Vich it's October, in course!'

133

I came upon a shrub with open, flat, white umbels; the actual flowers not unlike a hydrangea's, but spaced more widely apart. I asked the girl what it was. She replied, 'English hazel.' (!!) I could see, from the leaves, that it certainly was of the hazel family. Wonder what it is? 'Does it bear nuts?' I asked. 'No.' Perhaps Clif will throw light on this, when I get home.

(*Later*: Clif thinks it was probably *Viburnum tomentosum*.)

The girl also showed me what she called a 'Marguerite convolvulus' – silver foliage, white flower: upright, perhaps one and a half feet high, free-standing – not a trailer or a climber. The flower certainly *was* convolvulus-like. I've never seen a free-standing convolvulus before! (Later identified as *Convolvulus cneorum*.)

Date palms side by side with Lombardy poplars. I returned to breakfast very happy. Later, we flew to Sydney.

2ND OCTOBER

An *embarras de richesses*! Sydney is full of beautiful trees and shrubs; some I know – more I don't. I'll single out two. The first is *Ficus microcarpa 'Hillii'*; Hill's weeping fig: a bit like a big ilex or bay tree, the leaves pointed oval (cuspidate), light green, glaucous, about three inches long, borne in thick, pendent sprays. The whole tree appears very rich in foliage, cool and sheltering: dark, rugged bark; a few aerial roots, but not many. It's much planted round Sydney, for shade and decoration. A graceful, noble tree.

The second is a very resplendent job: *Bauhinia blakeana*. This – the orchid tree – is a *leguminosa*. I picked a spray growing over a garden wall, but it soon withered. The orchid-like, mauve-pink blossoms are about two inches in diameter, borne in long clusters (no scent). They have five overlapping petals and long, delicate, curving stamens like a hibiscus. Apart from the beauty of the blooms, the leaves are very attractive and unusual. They are twin-lobed, about five inches in diameter and pale green, with conspicuous veins running the length of the leaf and a deep cleft at the further end (so that they look a bit like a playing-card heart).

twin-lobed leaves of the ~ Bauhinia blakeana

Apparently this 'Hong Kong orchid tree' was unknown to Europeans until the eighteenth century, when it was named Bauhinea after two sixteenth-century brothers Bauhin, who were botanists. (Twin-lobed leaf, see?) There are several varieties of Bauhinea, e.g. *variegata*, *blakeana*, *variegata alba*, *purpurea*, *hookeri*, etc. This find quite made the day.

3RD OCTOBER

To-day we went to Canberra, a city laid out like a huge park. For lunch we ate sandwiches in the Botanical Gardens, where we saw the spectacular Superb Blue wren, *Malurus cyaneus*. This one was rather tame – no doubt from living in the gardens – and flew quite happily within a few feet of us. The head is a brilliant, royal blue, varied with black; the long, upward-cocked tail is also blue, the wings brown, belly whitish. In habit and behaviour it's very like our wren, frequenting hedges and bushes; though this one also kept popping in and out of clumps of rushes in a pond. There are a great many Australian wrens – about sixteen altogether, though some are rare and found only in relatively small areas, e.g. the mallee emu-wren.

4TH OCTOBER

Grevillea aquifolium is a large shrub, often grown to form tall hedges. Its 'leaves' are needles, much like those of a pine or fir, borne on long, springy branches. (The family is Proteaceae and there are about 200 different species.) It has conspicuous, deep-red flowers of a tufty appearance, so that to an Englishman it is somewhat reminiscent of a larch. The 'needles', however, are much darker, like a cedar's. I don't know whether it bears cones. It *looks* like a conifer, red blooms or no.

5TH OCTOBER

Prostanthera sieber is a biggish bush, purple-flowering, and has an attractive, mint-like scent when the leaves are bruised. It can only be a mint, I think – biggest member of the family I've ever seen.

I've failed to identify a perky little bird – possibly a fantail of some kind – grey with a hint of red round the eye; active and rather tame. It must be in the book, but I can't find it.

We drove about forty miles out of Sydney to the Hawkesbury river at Berowra. Here it runs in a deep, sheer gorge of yellow rock, about 200 to 300 yards across. Plenty of boats; and a few dwellings along the shore. Nevertheless, it is a rural, secluded place. Although it's about thirty-eight miles from the sea, it is tidal, we were told. I saw cormorants fishing. They were recognizably cormorants, though somewhat different in appearance from those in our home waters. Perhaps these are inland dwellers, like *Anhinga anhinga* in Florida.

When you pass through open country round Sydney, you get a vivid idea of what the early settlers contended with. It's steep and thickly wooded, with many deep (say 400 feet), precipitous gorges winding all ways. It's difficult to imagine how anyone in the nineteenth century could cross such country or 'tame' it. In these gorges the light changes continually throughout the day.

Anigozanthos manglesii, the kangaroo paw: an impressive if grotesque wild flower, a good four feet tall, the bloom bright red and bright green, curved and clubbed at the end of its long stalk, so that it really does much resemble an animal's paw.

Anigozanthos manglesii

6TH OCTOBER

In the Sydney Botanical Gardens. *Brunfelsia brasiliensis* (var. *acuminata*) – one of the Solanaceae, if you please! – must be one of the most attractive shrubs in the world. It forms a good, big bush, fully six feet tall or a little more, and at this time of year – spring – is entirely covered with bloom; five-petalled, each about the size of a hydrangea blossom; some white, some purple! It is actually bi-coloured, having purple blooms and white blooms on the same shrub. It is very fragrant, the scent a bit like *Viburnum fragrans*. You can smell it from ten feet away. The pointed leaves are light green, about one and a half or two inches long, in appearance rather like privet leaves.

Another Solanacea – very different – is *Jachroma warscewiczii*, which is Peruvian. This has pendent, deep-purple, tubular flowers in drooping clusters of two and three, curled open like little trumpets and each about two and a half inches long. The purple colour is so deep that the shrub looks a bit mournful, really – the blooms hanging vertically, all still in the bright sunshine. It grows to a height of about seven feet.

We flew to Adelaide this evening, arriving after heavy rain.

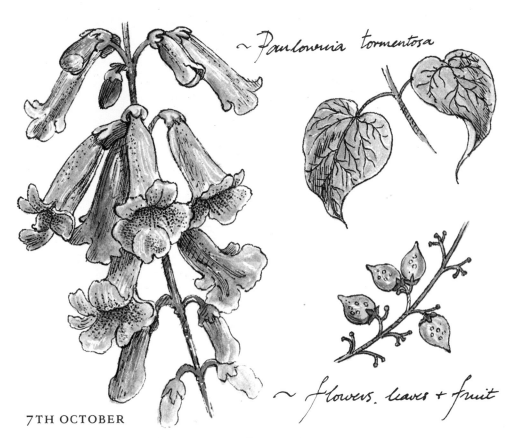

~ Paulownia tormentosa

~ flowers, leaves + fruit

7TH OCTOBER

To-day I have seen one of the most beautiful trees I have ever seen in my life – the Empress tree. Family, Bignoniaceae. Species, *Paulownia tomentosa*. This particular one was about twenty-five or thirty feet tall, symmetrical, with a graceful, relatively slender, smooth trunk and regular branches. The leaves are heart-shaped, veined, rather like those of a lime, and distinctly sticky. The tree was covered with trumpet-shaped flowers, five-petalled at the mouths (two petals above and three below), shaped something like, but larger than, those of our yellow mimulus. These blooms were each about two inches long, arranged in opposite pairs, six or seven pairs to a cluster along the stalk. They are heliotrope in colour, but inside their mouths have a pale-yellow flush, lightly maculated deep purple. The scent is delicate and fragrant. The sight of this tree, covered with its pale-mauve, trumpet-shaped blooms, is a fair knockout.

(*Later*: I'm advised that it is practicable to grow the tree in Great Britain, so I shall try. I fear it may not flower so profusely, however.)

8TH OCTOBER

Brisbane is very hot. Empress trees in bloom everywhere: likewise poinsettia with its great, scarlet leaves. The Australian greenfinch (at least, I think that's what it must be – no Australian seems to know the name of any bird or flower when asked) has a black eye-stripe like an English willow warbler, and a white collar like an English stonechat.

If only Australia weren't so far away, blest if I wouldn't live there, buy sixty acres and make a garden! In this climate you couldn't go wrong. Everything thrives; everything burgeons. The trees alone are enough to wring your heart – gums, yellow-flowering wattles (mimosa), eucalyptus, figs and many more, all of the greatest nobility.

9TH OCTOBER

Landed at Heathrow. Returned to the Isle of Man in the evening. The martins and swallows are all gone, of course.

10TH OCTOBER

At 7.30 a.m. the first thing I see is that damned heron standing in the lake as if he owned the place! He's had it to himself for eighteen days, too. Wonder whether I've got any golden orfe left? They keep fairly deep in colder weather, of course. Can only hope for the best.

11TH OCTOBER

Walking with Stewart. Coming down a lane into Agneash, Tetter was most viciously set upon by a yellow Labrador, which got him down and was actually tearing his throat – it would have killed him, I'm convinced – when Stewart, with unhesitating resolution and courage, laid hold of it. It had no collar, and Stewart, since he could therefore get no purchase on its neck, straddled it, bent over and grabbed it by the two front paws – thereby exposing himself to being bitten in either hand – and hauled it bodily upward. As it didn't let go of Tetter's throat, he came up too. Stewart then banged the side of the Labrador's head with his elbow. When it had finally let go, Stewart kept it in check with his stick, while Tetter made off down the lane. Neither Stewart nor Tetter was wounded, but great hanks of Tetter's coat were out and he was shaken and subdued for some time after.

As savage and alarming a dog-fight as ever I've seen in my life. Stewart's conduct was beyond praise, and certainly saved Tetter's life.

12TH OCTOBER

A fine autumn day, with the Mountains of Mourne very clear across the Irish Sea, as often in October. Most of the leaves are gone from the big ash tree.

Down by the lake found a pretty, small antirrhinum, purple and pale yellow, with filiform leaves. Cannot trace it in Keble Martin or Fitter and Fitter, so it can only be a garden escape. I think it is *Linaria purpurea*.

I've now seen golden orfe in the lake, so *Ardea cinerea* (the heron) hasn't had them all, anyway.

18TH OCTOBER

The willow warblers – always the latest-remaining of the migrant Silviidae – have gone. But this afternoon I saw another grey wagtail – this time on my own lake. Although the leaves are still on the trees I feel conscious, out walking, of the autumnal *emptying* of the land – of birds, insects and the standing corn. The effect is to enlarge the sky, which stretches in a vast, cool, remote canopy from one horizon to another, full of clouds and much bigger than the land. One walks *under* the sky rather than *through* the land.

139

19TH OCTOBER

A perfect October day – bright sunshine, no wind, turning leaves, the air clear and chill and the sea very blue. Scotland, Ireland and the Lake District clearly visible.

Crossed to London in the evening.

20TH OCTOBER

The leaves are hanging on late this year. Walking in sunshine and windless air in St James's Park, I found myself in what felt and looked like a forest of gold and bronze trees, between which, at a little distance, one caught glimpses of a still, green river – the lake. I came upon what I take to have been a weeping hazel. I suppose there is such a thing? Must ask Clif.

Syon House —

21ST OCTOBER (*Trafalgar Day*)

The fine weather still holds. Business all day, but one thing happened which was rather pleasing. Walking up Marylebone High Street, I suddenly saw a heron overhead, fairly high. It was going north-eastward, so I suppose it was making for the Tottenham reservoirs or the Hackney Marshes, having come, perhaps, from the Syon House area. I feel more charitable towards herons here than I do when they're prospecting my lake!

22ND OCTOBER

To-day we drove from London up to Gisburn, in Yorkshire. Bedfordshire and Huntingdon were misty, their flat fields stretching away into vague, white distance which, as we reached Lincolnshire later in the afternoon, changed to flying mirk and a gradual breaking-up of the fine weather. We stopped off near Sandy, and here I saw a Siberian crab-apple tree, covered with round fruit red as cherries, on the edge of a commercial nursery garden's field of outdoor chrysanthemums.

We reached Gisburn soon after six. How nice to arrive, as darkness falls, at a place where you're welcome – to have a drink and a chat before bath and dinner! Homer liked that, and people have been enjoying it ever since.

23RD OCTOBER (*Alamein Day*)

Weather tempestuous; wind howling and leaves all round the hotel.

Returning to London this afternoon, we drove beside first the Aire and then the Wharfe. Both were in high, brown-yellow flood, over their banks, the watery fields full of gulls and plovers. Ilkley Moor, high to the south, looked bleak and sodden. Tha would certainly catch thee death of cold, I thought. We approached Arthington down yellow, tossing avenues of lime, sycamore and beech. The evening came out fine, however, with a cloudy, ochre and pale-green sunset over Lincolnshire. Newark spire standing dark against a russet and yellow sky in the west. Later a full moon rose in a calm sky beyond St Ives.

25TH OCTOBER

Woken in the night by the honking and clamour of geese. Got up and looked out into Hyde Park – a woodland of plane trees, not forty yards distant. No geese to be seen, yet the cries were everywhere, far and near, and continued for some time. Too many to be attributable merely to the resident population of the Serpentine. Some migration?

26TH OCTOBER (*Sunday*)

The clocks went back last night. Winter again! This particular day has been cold, too, just to rub it in.

In the afternoon Elizabeth and I drove down from London to Little Coxwell, near Faringdon, to see Richard and Audrey Ryder. A bright, still, sunny afternoon. I can't remember a more beautiful autumn.

I was pleased, while walking round the village with Richard at dusk, to see a house almost entirely covered in Virginia creeper; a deep, autumnal red, the big leaves cernuous in the evening wind. I know it's common enough, but it's one of the seasonal things I enjoy. I believe I'm right in thinking that only Virginia creeper and ivy will cling to a wall unsupported. Of those two, give me Virginia creeper every time!

(*Later*: There is a climbing hydrangea that will, too.)

30TH OCTOBER

Flew back to the Isle. Nearly all the leaves are off the trees. The Switchback is once more a high, wind-exposed terrace – no longer a leafy tunnel.

The bonsai elm is shedding its leaves, which have already turned.

31ST OCTOBER (*Friday*)

Well, here's Hallowe'en, and an end to all the summer – the warblers and terns; and the wild flowers – or most of them. It's a dull, fine morning – bare trees or brown leaves; and a calm, pale-blue sea with a slight mist. An autumnal smell in the soil and trees, wet and leafy. I've been carrying in logs for the library fire.

Two Manx folk-rhymes for Hallowe'en. They call it 'Hop tu naa' (pronounced 'nay') here. The children come round – turnip lanterns, etc.

> 1. 'Hop tu naa! Hop tu naa!
>   Jinny the Witch flew over the house
>   To get a stick to lather the mouse.
>   Hop tu naa! Hop tu naa!'

2. 'Hop tu naa, ringo, ringo!
   Hop tu naa, I've burnt my fingo!
   Ladies and gentlemen sitting by the fire,
   And us poor creatures out in the mire!
   If you're going to give us anything, give it us soon,
   'Cos we're going home by the light of the moon.'

Richard Arnold (our instructor on the Bangor sea-bird course) arrived to stay the week-end.

November

1ST NOVEMBER

The first thing Richard Arnold and I saw this morning was a redwing (*Turdus iliacus*) in the hawthorn tree, eating the berries: the yellow supercilium (eye-stripe) very plain.

This afternoon Stewart, Richard and I walked from Peel to Glenmaye along the cliff. There were plenty of choughs, which pleased Richard. He pointed out a couple of peregrines (*Falco peregrinus*) over the coastal meadows. Watching one through binoculars, what struck me was the upward-curving shape of the wings in flight; and in general, the *burly* appearance of the bird.

— redwing —

2ND NOVEMBER

My bonsai elm should correctly be called *Zelkova serrata*, Richard says.

Pam Ayres came to lunch. Most amusing. She recited a poem she'd just made up, about the horrors of having other people's children visiting. It was hugely risible.

After discussing the question of duck for the lake, we've decided to wait a year, until the surrounding land has been planted. At the moment the edges are still so bare that Richard thinks there's a risk that duck, brought in now, might wander away in search of cover.

144

A flock of fieldfares (*Turdus pilaris*) went over the house this morning. We can expect to have fieldfares around from now on.

3RD NOVEMBER

Clear, bright and cold. On a wet, sheltered bank I came upon a stunted plant of what I believe to be Devil's bit scabious (*Succisa pratensis*) blooming late. 'Damp places; elliptical, untoothed leaves.'

Richard Arnold left.

Here is a charming sonnet on November by Hartley Coleridge, son of Samuel Taylor Coleridge. Hartley, a rather pathetic figure, died of bronchitis in 1849 at the age of fifty-three.

> 'The mellow year is hasting to its close;
> The little birds have almost sung their last.
> Their small notes twitter in the dreary blast –
> That shrill-piped harbinger of early snows.
> The patient beauty of the scentless rose,
> Oft with the morn's hoar crystal quaintly glass'd,
> Hangs, a pale mourner for the summer past,
> And makes a little summer where it grows.
> In the chill sunbeam of the faint, brief day,
> The dusky waters shudder as they shine,
> The russet leaves obstruct the straggling way
> Of oozy brooks, which no deep banks define,
> And the gaunt woods, in ragged, scant array,
> Wrap their old limbs with sombre ivy twine.'

4TH NOVEMBER

This is the season when the Manx hold their 'Melliahs'. A Melliah, in my view, is rather an improvement on Harvest Festival. The kindly fruits of the earth are taken not to church but to the local, where they are displayed. Then, on the Melliah evening, there is a well-attended beer-up, at which everyone, including the vicar (who starts the proceedings with a bit of an informal service and a few prayers), has a jolly time and gets high. Afterwards, the produce is auctioned and the proceeds given to charity.

~ devil's bit Scabious

5TH NOVEMBER

Bonfires and Beltane all over the Island! I've always enjoyed Guy

Fawkes night. I fear many cats and dogs don't, though. Fire remains the great dividing line between humans and other animals. Question: 'When did Man cease to be an ape and become human?' Answer: 'When he learned to control and use fire.'

'For the burning of sins and winter.' I've tried to trace this quotation, but can't.

6TH NOVEMBER

Roy Greenwood (a model for the Rev. Tony Redwood in *The Girl in a Swing*) is here from his Lake District parsonage for a day or two. An excellent walk with him this afternoon, finishing by climbing the very steep west slope of Cronk ny Arrey Laa. Roy's very fit. 'I hope you didn't mind having to hold back a bit on my account,' I said as we reached the car in twilight. 'Not at all,' replied Roy. 'The sight of your backside going up ahead of me on hands and knees was ample compensation.'

Roy wants to find out more about the little *keeills*, or ruined chapels (any date from eighth to fourteenth century), found about the Island. Must investigate.

7TH NOVEMBER

This is a season of noticing little things in a landscape daily barer and barer. The resident missel-thrush is most aggressive. I have two or three times observed him chasing blackbirds off the property. Smaller birds he leaves alone.

Roy left to-day, vowing to return in spring. Said he'd had no idea the Island was so beautiful.

8TH NOVEMBER

I've been watching once again the goldcrests in the pines along the north border of Knocksharry. They never keep still for a moment, pecking and fluttering, and show up beautifully against the sombre, dark-green pine-needles.

9TH NOVEMBER

Prunus subhirtella ('*Autumnalis*') is in bloom by the Union Mills cross-roads. I had one in my garden in London. It used to excite comment among the Islingtonians by blooming at this time of year, extending branches of flounced, pale-pink blossom over the wall, often in bitter cold.

10TH NOVEMBER

Clif thinks my 'weeping hazel' in St James's Park (20th October) must actually be a weeping *elm*. There is, it seems, a 'contorted hazel', but not a weeping one.

11TH NOVEMBER

The pink aubretia is in bloom all along the front flower-bed. I'm a bit surprised, for the weather has been much colder this last few days.

12TH NOVEMBER

Surprised, coming back to Knocksharry after dark this evening, to come upon a hedgehog picked out by my headlights. I should have thought it would be in hibernation by now. It was only just outside the gate, so I carried it in and let it go on the edge of the wood. Let's hope it takes up residence.

13TH NOVEMBER

Driving over to pick up Janice this morning, I passed a fair-sized flock of redwings on the telegraph wires near Ballamona.

16TH NOVEMBER

This afternoon – a typical November afternoon, rather windy, not too cold, but cloudy, with darkness beginning to fall before half past four – I came upon an elder tree with an attractive, jelly-looking fungus growing on it: in colour a livid dark red, domed and rubbery, in discs.

Brightman and Nicholson, *The Oxford Book of Flowerless Plants*, identify this as *Auricularia auricula*, 'ear fungus'. 'Especially common in autumn and almost entirely restricted to elder. Varies from livid brown to a dark flesh colour. Irregularly saucer-shaped, with inrolled margins and surfaces thrown into shallow, irregular folds. Outer surface very finely velvety, flesh slightly translucent, feeling rather like very soft and flexible rubber.'

What an excellent description – comprehensive, graphic and precise! The family is Tremellales, jelly fungi. About fifty species are found in Britain.

– *auricularia auricula* –

17TH NOVEMBER

Very high wind again – a nor'-wester this time, howling on into the night. The magpies (plentiful as tabby cats, in point of fact, too many) seem undeterred by any amount of wind. They take to the air in the gale, balancing with the help of their long tails, which they can partly open, and raise or lower almost to a right angle. I don't care for them – raffish, predatory creatures; 'can't sing, either.

18TH NOVEMBER

Near Blue Point this afternoon, on the north-west coast, I saw three or four twites (*Acanthis flavirostris*). Dr Philip Burton describes the twite as 'a more northerly counterpart of the linnet' (*Acanthis cannabina*). They like moors and heather and don't, I gather, come south of the midlands much. I wouldn't back myself to tell a female twite and a female linnet apart, especially in the rain, which darkens plumage. But a male twite is easier to distinguish, having no red crown or red breast and not being chestnut on the back. The difficult thing is that he *behaves* very much like a linnet, and so often all you have to go on is behaviour.

22ND NOVEMBER

Janice, being Manx, calls wood-lice 'parson's pigs' – a delightful vernacular term. I've no more objection to wood-lice than to earwigs. I looked for them in Michael Chinery and then in Jiri

Zahradnik. No luck – they're not insects! The *O.E.D.* says: 'A small isopod crustacean of the sub-order Oniscoidea.' The common wood-louse is *Armadillidium*. An isopod is 'an animal of the order of sessile-eyed crustaceans, characterized by seven pairs of equal and similarly placed thoracic legs; comprising marine, freshwater and terrestrial species, some being parasitic'. Sessile, in this context, seems to mean 'adhering close to the surface' or perhaps 'immediately attached by the base'.

25TH NOVEMBER

The fulmars are back! Spot on time, too, according to Dr Philip Burton, who says they 'return to the breeding cliffs in November or December from extensive wanderings in the North Atlantic'. It'll be the recent storms, I suppose, that have turned them shoreward. They don't breed until May, but they'll be around the Island from now on.

28TH NOVEMBER

The first snow! It has been bitterly cold, with sleet last night on a driving north-west wind; and this morning, in the cold, clear, sunny weather, the Mountains of Mourne appear shining white, almost indistinguishable from the cumulus clouds on the horizon. There's snow on *our* hills, too. The Greeba Ridge is a beautiful sight in the sunshine.

29TH NOVEMBER

A rampant, burgeoning umbellifer on the verge of the Switchback. It's a wild carrot, I am fairly sure (*Daucus carota*). Keble Martin gives the blooming period as June to August and Fitter as June to September. This one's covered with new umbels in bud!

Various things are in full bloom in sheltered places – notably primroses and the red wall-valerian.

30TH NOVEMBER

And Clif Dadd calls wood-lice 'crawley-buttons!' (Ref. 22nd November.) I think Geoffrey Grigson ought to follow up his *Englishman's Flora* with an *Englishman's Insects*. Insects have different vernacular names all over the place. My nanny (nursery-maid, *not* grandmother) used to call daddy-long-legs 'plim-ploms'; I suppose from the way in which they bounce on and off light-bulbs. And cockchafers were 'dumbledores' to Thomas Hardy.

daucus carota –

Knockshany under snow

December

1ST DECEMBER

The night sky is splendid these evenings – it's very cold just now (the lake was lightly iced over this morning) with the winter constellations once more rising early. Aldebaran (Taurus) and Gemini are up, over the hill to the east of the house, by nine o'clock.

2ND DECEMBER

Down the east side of the Island, they've had a migration of blackbirds. 'A migration of *blackbirds*?' I asked Clif sceptically. 'It can only be,' he replied. 'We normally have no blackbirds, or very few, in Ballalheanagh Glen. The raptors take them. One day I saw a merlin actually take a blackbird. It was only the size of the blackbird itself.'

4TH DECEMBER

Walked on the Ayres in shocking weather, and for my pains saw quite a sizeable flock of redshanks. They have a curious flight-behaviour, difficult to describe – sort of wavering – which makes them easy to identify at a distance even if you can't see the plumage. When you disturb them they kick up an awful shine. The book says they come inland for food when it gets too cold for the *Corophia* (small crustaceans) to show themselves out of the maritime mud. However, I've never seen any yet at Knocksharry.

6TH DECEMBER

Knapweed, nipplewort and red campion all blooming along the Switchback.

7TH DECEMBER

Frost in the night, and to-day cat-ice everywhere, not melting in the bright, blue-skied, sunny cold. A lovely day for walking and walk we did, Tetter and I, along the cliffs. I've often thought it remarkable that there's only one kind of wild ivy (Araliacea) in this country, to wit, *Hedera helix*, which I've reviled so bitterly all through this diary. There's a poem about it by Thomas Hardy, characteristically ironical and bitter. The ivy says it tried a beech, but that was no good: then a plane and that was no good. Finally it tried an ash, and that was marvellous – until the ash fell and died as a result.

The white umbels of the ivy bloom late, in October and November, and just now the fruit is setting in pale-green blobs. There are two kinds of leaf; the dark-green, three-pointed kind everyone knows, and the pale-green, oval kind that grow on the shoots which flower.

10TH DECEMBER

A beautiful, starry night with a clear moon, a little older than new. It's a 'crescent' moon until it's over the 'half'. Between half and full it's 'gibbous' – splendid word! (Latin, *'gibbus'* = a hump. Hence 'convex, rounded, protuberant'.) Tetter and I went for a starlit walk. If you didn't look directly at where it was, you could just see the glimmer of the Great Andromeda nebula, high in the east. Its light takes 2 million years to reach the earth, travelling at 186,000 miles a second. I never know whether this is encouraging or otherwise. On the one hand, nothing matters much. On the other, what's the use of bothering about anything?

12TH DECEMBER

A stormy day of high wind and rain. Knocksharry this morning was full of curlews calling and balancing on the wind. The field below was black with rooks, grey with hooded crows and white with gulls.

13TH DECEMBER

It's rather odd that there's been no mention, throughout this diary, of the Giant's Fingers. About half to three-quarters of a mile south of Knocksharry and well up on the hillside above it, at the top of an extensive area of gorse-grown waste land, stand (or rather, lie) eight rough blocks of white feldspar (silicate of alumina with soda, potash, lime, etc.). These (although there are actually eight of them) are the Giant's Fingers. Two are about two-thirds as big (though not as high) as a small car, four are perhaps half as big as a small car, and two are much smaller. The area of the whole group is about thirty-three by eighteen feet.

The Giant's Fingers are not an artefact. The stones, I'm informed, were moved and deposited by glacial action. They may not, in fact, have come very far, for local farmers, when ploughing, or digging for some particular purpose, e.g. laying foundations for a shed, still come upon great lumps of this feldspar well down in the ground. They tend to 'come up' from time to time, but sink again.

The white stones show clearly above the gorse from the Peel to Kirk Michael road about a mile to seaward. From that viewpoint, they certainly are reminiscent of four fingers and an extended thumb.

14TH DECEMBER

Twilight at four o'clock, dark by twenty to five. Cold, too. I'm delighted to find that a sentence from *Watership Down* appears in *The Penguin Dictionary of Modern Quotations*. 'Many human beings say that they enjoy the winter, but what they really enjoy is feeling proof against it.' Yes, indeed. Glad I'm not a rabbit at this time of year.

15TH DECEMBER

This morning, in the road outside the Manx Arms at Onchan, I saw something I can't remember to have seen before; an albino jackdaw. He was among several other jackdaws, pecking about in the road. He had conspicuous white stripes down the wings. The other jackdaws seemed to accept him all right. I dare say albinoism occurs in all the corvines, to some extent, as well as in blackbirds.

I remember seeing, also, an albino coot on the river Test in Hampshire.

albino jackdaw

16TH DECEMBER

This afternoon a high gale – a sou'-wester, as usual. Walking on the cliffs north of Peel, I watched the herring gulls playing an odd game. The waves were coming in high, breaking with considerable force. There were, however, quite long intervals between each wave. Flocks of gulls were sitting on the sea about fifty yards out, all facing into the wind. As each wave reached them, they rode up on it, but would not remain to ride the crest. Just before the moment when they would have found themselves topping the crest, they invariably took to their wings, flew up and over the white cap and alighted again on the long swell on the further side. They kept this up for as long as I was walking on the cliffs and watching them. Elizabeth said, 'Do you suppose they keep it up all night?' I dare say they very well might. It's a form of 'loitering', after all.

17TH DECEMBER

Saw a small flock of purple sandpipers (*Calidris maritima*) on the rocks below Peel Castle. It's a favourite haunt of theirs in winter months.

purple sandpipers —

18TH DECEMBER

Along the boundary between Knocksharry House and the Switchback lane which runs beside it on the eastern (landward) side, the previous owner planted a belt of Monterey cypress (*Cupressus macrocarpa*). These make quite a good wind-belt, standing thickly together. They're now about fourteen feet tall. The trouble is, Clif tells me, that they tend to lean to leeward after a time and then to keel over altogether. (But they're cheap to buy.) I think I'll replace them and get something a bit more reliable (and beautiful). They ought to burn well, at least!

19TH DECEMBER

In bloom in many gardens all over the Island just now is *Schizostylis coccinea*, the kaffir lily. A split style and a pink or red bloom. Brightens up the winter quite a bit!

20TH DECEMBER

A beautifully mild, windless day. Dropping in at Clif's gardens, I saw two pleasing things in bloom. The big mahonias, which look rather like holly, only with pinnate leaves. They have bright-yellow sprays of bloom, very fragrant. Also *Primula whitei*, the Himalayan primula: an ice-blue bloom, very beautiful. How Shakespeare (or Herrick or Keats for that matter) would have loved winter cheered up by these exotic plants! I wonder what there'll be in another four hundred years? Climate control, perhaps; or instant travel. Half an hour in an Australian garden by means of hallucinatory thought-transference? That's no stranger than wireless would have seemed to Socrates.

21ST DECEMBER

The winter solstice; shortest day. No sun whatever to be seen throughout the entire day.

> ''Tis the yeares midnight, and it is the dayes,
> Lucies, who scarce seven houres herself unmaskes.
> The Sunne is spent, and now his flaskes
> Send forth light squibs, no constant rayes;
> The world's whole sap is sunke:
> The general balme th' hydroptique earth hath drunk.'

John Donne was doing better than we. We haven't even had any light squibs.

22ND DECEMBER

Hamamelis mollis, the witch-hazel, is a splendid winter-blooming shrub! Beautiful, feathery, yellow rosettes, and the sharp-sweet scent so fresh and pleasant.

'*Hamamelis virginica*, known as witch-hazel, is native to North America. The bark and leaves are astringent and the seeds contain oil and are edible. The name derives from the use of the twigs as divining rods, just as hazel twigs are used in England.' (*Enc. Brit.*)

24TH DECEMBER

The bonsai elm has shed its last leaves. It's still healthy and thriving. I must say, they're very easy to look after.

25TH DECEMBER (*Christmas Day*)

King Arthur, the reader will recall, used to say, on great feast days, that he would not sit down to meat until he had heard or seen of a great marvel. (See e.g. Malory, beginning of Book VII.) The great marvel always duly turned up and the dinner was never spoilt. I thought I'd try this, and went for a walk up Glen Helen. What I saw were a great many plants of the lesser celandine (*Ranunculus ficaria*) coming on strong for next year. No buds yet, but a lot of new leaves. In that sheltered place they probably *will* be in bloom soon. Good enough to justify sitting down to Christmas dinner, anyway.

27TH DECEMBER

Perfect December weather to-day; no wind at all and quite warm, with a sky intermittently lightly cloudy. Wet earth, pine-woods and leaves all smelling beautiful. Stewart and I walked from Onchan through Molly Quirk's Glen, up the lane to the Kerrowdhoo reservoir and then past Clypse, the higher reservoir. From there we went up the muddy lonnin to Honeyhill and so to the Laxey road about half a mile east of Creg-ny-Baa. We did the best part of two miles eastward, past Conrhenny Plantation, and so dropped steeply down into Glen Roy, over the stream in the woods at the bottom and as steeply up again to Baldhoon: and thence down to the Mines Tavern at Laxey. I suppose it might be seven miles. The good weather made it very enjoyable. We finished in the dark, of course.

Julie and Peter arrived in the evening, in great form.

28TH DECEMBER

To-day I was quoting the old folk-rhyme for 26th December:

> 'The wren, the wren, the king of all birds,
> St Stephen's Day was slain in the furze.'

'That's all wrong,' said Janice. 'We don't sing that here on the Island.' She then gave me the following, for the same occasion:

> '"We hunt the wren," says Robin the Bobbin.
> "We hunt the wren," says Christopher Robin.
> "We hunt the wren," says Jack of the Land.
> "We hunt the wren," says everyone.'

Frazer's *Golden Bough*, Chapter 54, is of interest here, for it gives both versions and refers specifically to the Isle of Man. ('Processions with Sacred Animals'.) But Janice's version, acquired orally of course, has undergone a change or two (e.g. 'Christopher Robin'). Frazer has 'Jack of the Can' for 'Jack of the Land'. (Phallic euphemisms?)

30TH DECEMBER

As the year draws to an end, what have we? Ash trees covered with bunches of 'keys' and also black buds; and bare larches covered all

along the boughs with little brown cones. In the front border a bloom of bugle, all of three inches tall and dusty blue. Primroses. And the dwarf cyclamen by the waterfall are all in leaf, but no blooms as yet.

Venus will be a bright morning star in January, rising two hours before the sun. No bright stars near it. Jupiter and Saturn will be close together on the 14th, visible at early evening. That should be a good sight, if we get clear weather.

31ST DECEMBER

red campion —

To-day I repeated the exercise I performed on 1st January last, and went out to see what might be in bloom. (It was blowing a high gale, but I staggered along in a balaclava, gloves and a heavy overcoat.) Celandines: a lot in bloom in sheltered, wet places. What pleases me here is that they're next year's flowers, not last year's. Also: one dark-red bloom of escallonia in the hedge opposite Knocksharry; gorse, of course, and ragwort (cushag), equally of course; a good deal of red campion; some scentless mayweed; wild carrot; a buttercup and a dandelion; some rather bedraggled moon-daisies; a healthy, ramping plant of shepherd's purse, covered in bloom; and in the cottage garden down Brack-a-Broom lane, a big clump of 'shot' wallflowers. In our garden two daffodils are in bud.

Wild flowers are like pubs. There are generally one or two open somewhere, if only you look hard enough. On that note this diary shall close, with Orion glittering bright and Sirius, near it, even brighter. It's so cold that the fire is burning very crisp and clear. I can hear the sea; I can hear the wind. I'm not hungry or cold or ill. What more should anyone want?

dandelion —